THE DIY GUIDE TO

CHARITY NEWSLETTERS

For Charities
Voluntary Organisations
and Community Groups

By Chris Wells

A DIRECTORY OF SOCIAL CHANGE PUBLICATION

The DIY Guide to Charity Newsletters

by Chris Wells

Published by the Directory of Social Change,
24 Stephenson Way, London NW1 2DP

The Directory of Social Change is registered
charity no. 800517

© 1996 Directory of Social Change

Designed by Linda Parker and Kate Bass
Printed and bound by Page Bros., Norwich

British Library Cataloguing in Publication Data.
A catalogue record for this book is available
from the British Library

ISBN 1 873860 11 0

Acknowledgements

The author wishes to thank the following people for their assistance
with this book: John Hodges, Barnabus Fellowship Worldwide;
Talking Sense; Mark Lattimer, Trust Monitor; Liz Shore, Medical Woman;
Liz Mather and Marcus Nissen, News Beat; Jackie Curtis, Childworld
(GB); Danny Smith, Jubilee Action; Richard Haycock, Concerning Age
Concern Enfield; Mo Houlder, Centrepoint; Brian Hammett, News From
The Dock.

About the author

Chris Wells is a training consultant who conducts around 100 seminars
and training days each year across the length and breadth of the
country. He has worked with many household names in both the charity
and business worlds on their publications and other training needs.

This book stems directly from delegate requests for more information
and guidelines on successful newsletters. When he's not lecturing his
family life is the number one priority. As Grace and Chris have eight
children, it's a pretty busy household!

Contents

ANYONE CAN WRITE A SIMPLE NEWSLETTER... CAN'T THEY?

Newsletters are one of the fastest growing methods of communication. The ability to produce limited print run material from your own desk top publishing system has increased their growth still further. In the charity sector, they are used extensively for maintaining communication with supporters and donors. In the business world, they are used for maintaining contact with customers. Staff newsletters are becoming popular in both sectors as they boost morale.

Any one of us can look around and spot several newsletters that are visited upon us both in our local community and at work. This often leads to the erroneous conclusion that newsletters are a 'good thing'.

Newsletters can be a good thing – but they can also contribute to the seemingly inevitable growth in junk mail. The ability to publish from your desk doesn't mean you will publish well. Even if you write brilliantly, the message can all too easily be lost in the presentation on the page.

This book tries to get you over some of the more difficult hurdles you will encounter with tips on design and editing, practical stories for editors, presentation and typographic clues. It also discusses some of the hurdles you haven't yet thought about; like what do your readers think of your efforts? Can you take advertising to cover the costs of publication? Should you promote a 'house style'?

The book won't, however, tell you if a newsletter is a good idea for your organisation. Or if you are the sort of person who will enjoy being an editor. Those are decisions that you must make once you've read it. But at least you'll be better informed about the realities of the task ahead.

In an era of specialist television and radio, the Internet and its host of modern communication techniques, are people more likely to download or listen in than read up? That depends, in the end, on the cohesiveness and abilities of your potential audience. But if you get it right, the very term **newsletter** will ensure readership.

A good newsletter should be a welcome, regular visitor, that can be relied upon for accurate, factual information not readily available from any other source. But if it is sent out to a variety of audiences with a number of objectives – it can't achieve that aim.

One of the problems of writing a book of this sort is being constantly on the look out for examples of good and bad practice. And, of course, weak examples are more common, and educationally more helpful, than good ones. So a very big thank you to all those brave souls who have taken the risk in letting us include their work in the book. I have tried to select examples that also show the variety of styles and approaches that work for different audiences.

Other thank yous must start with Grace, without whose support nothing is possible, and include Linda Parker, Kate Bass and Anne Mountfield at the Directory of Social Change. And Audrey Semple, for allowing me to borrow heavily from her Sell Space to Make Money for the contents of Chapter 9.

If each and every one of you who reads this book can find one good idea to help improve your newsletter, it will have been worth it.

CHAPTER ONE

WHY PUBLISH A NEWSLETTER ?

Do you need a newsletter?

Most charity newsletters are produced by a member of staff as one aspect of their job. A few are produced by a volunteer or team of volunteers. Most are there because somebody, somewhere, lost in the mists of time, thought it was a 'good idea to keep in touch'. You, the editor, were the person who was visiting the toilet when the 'good idea' came looking for a home. So, before you read any further, stop and ask yourself a simple question: *'Does my charity need a newsletter?'*

Newsletters are most successful when providing regular information to a specific audience with a common interest. Normally relaxed and informal in style, they will contain a number of short articles and have a limited shelf or coffee table life. Very few newsletters are filed, kept, or read from cover to cover. Most are dipped into for short periods of time over a few days or a week or two – and end up in the waste paper basket.

This sense of regular, renewable contact is what is most attractive to charities in their newsletters, keeping donors, supporters, volunteers, and other key audiences aware of your activities and the positive results that can only happen because of their efforts and contributions. The key element is action.

What action do your readers want to hear about from your newsletter, and how will this affect them?

Pre-conditions for a successful newsletter

■ ACCESS – TO THE EDITOR AND THE CHARITY
Newsletters work best as a personal communication. They are seen as trusted purveyors of information creating an individual contact between the charity and the reader. A part of this trust is knowing who the editor is, how to contact them easily, and how the newsletter reflects the liveliness, personality and humour of this individual.

- What is the purpose of your newsletter?
- How often do readers contact you directly?
- What other communication is there with supporters?
- Does your newsletter contain news?

Chartown BULLETIN

Hello Chartown

This newsletter is distributed bi-monthly to the residents of Chartown and Vosley by the Keystone Charity and associated organisations.

Use your opportunities to talk directly to your readers

Wanted – new stories for old Editor

It's a lonely job being Editor of Talking Sense. Every three months, people suddenly start avoiding you. Phone calls go unreturned; letters unanswered.

Now even Members' News is giving me the cold shoulder. So, I'm making a small plea – please make an old Editor happy by sending her your contributions for this page. News from or about Sense's beneficiaries – new or old – is always welcome, and may give support to other readers.

The editors and their character are essential elements for the successful newsletter

This sense of open access and belonging underscores the importance of the link between reader and publisher. This also means the information in a newsletter is much more highly prized than that in newspapers and magazines. Readers need to feel they can check out the content directly with the editor if need be. Sometimes they just want to comment. You ignore or deny this process of exchanging views and information at your peril. It is the contact that maintains the common interest and commitment, and is the very life blood of the newsletter.

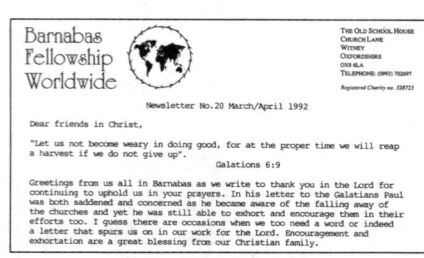

A common interest and single purpose are more important than graphic trickery

■ COMMON INTEREST

The content and the readership should have *a common and narrow sphere of interest.* Newsletters work best when working to a single, simple purpose. A mixed, perhaps confused, purpose will give a mixed and weaker message. It is always better and more effective to publish two newsletters each to influence a different audience than 'make do' with one for both groups.

■ CURRENT NEWS AND TOPICAL INFORMATION

The best newsletters convey a touch of *urgency*. Their content relates to the last few or next few weeks – matching the writing style to the 'shelf life' of the product. This 'currency' requirement will often dictate your frequency of publication.

■ PRINT IS THE MOST APPROPRIATE MEDIUM

Print is *not the only way* to communicate with your supporters. There are many other ways of keeping 'in touch' – posters, radio, television etc. Is the message best suited to that unique blend of information ('news') and personal contact ('letter') that the title 'newsletter' implies?

Should you be publishing a newsletter?

If you can identify in your charity an audience where print is the only sensible medium to reach it, and where that audience has a unique common interest, and an appetite for current information, then perhaps you should read on. A newsletter may be for your charity.

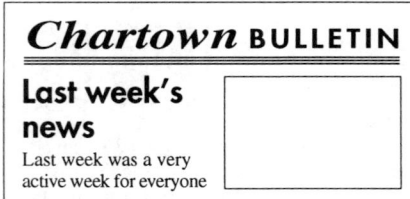

Newsletters must be timely and relevant

More importantly, if you already publish a newsletter and it doesn't fit the criteria, is the publication really necessary? Is it as effective as it could be? Each issue takes much time and effort to produce. Is it worth it? Or is it continuing to be published simply because *'it's always been there?'*

One charity found it had a problem with its printing and mailing house. For two issues the print run for their newsletter had been short, and on each occasion the final 12% of mailsort post codes had not been sent out. The problem came to light when the spare address labels were returned to the charity. But no reader complained. To none of these readers did the newsletter have enough current common interest for them to miss it.

When training or consulting I am often asked by harassed editors-*'How do I know if my newsletter is read?'* My answer is always the same. *'Delay your next issue by two weeks or so. If your telephone rings with inquiries there is no problem'.* Few have the courage to risk the silence.

What this book aims to do for you

The aim of this book is twofold. Firstly to improve your current or planned newsletter. To do that you should also look at successful and unsuccessful newsletters and magazines published by others. Analyse what you think makes them work, and what general guidelines you can deduce from them.

You will find many ideas in the pages of this book to refresh your newsletter and keep your readers looking forward even more eagerly to its arrival. If you're just starting out there is guidance here to help you on the right road to producing the best possible newsletter for your budget.

Secondly, the book aims to make the process of publishing your newsletter an easier task for you, the editor. Rarely is the newsletter your sole task; rather you will find 'editor' is just one of the many hats you wear each year. If there are ways to reduce the time and effort that you have to put into this job, it's hardly a crime!

Still want to write a newsletter? Then let's look first at planning for publication...

Here are a few simple questions which should help with the decision

- Have you an audience with sufficient numbers to justify the printing costs?
- Is there a single common interest, or a variety of messages and sub-groups to match up?
- Is there enough interesting information to tell the readers?
- Have you the time and energy needed for the regular cycle most newsletters require?
- How will this blend with the organisation's other communications?

Chartown BULLETIN

Editor arrested for easy existence "I didn't work hard enough"

The Editor of a very well known newsletter has been arrested for his

Being an editor, a whole new role in life!

Now Decide...

- What is the purpose of your newsletter?
- How often do readers contact you directly?
- What other communication is there with supporters?
- Does your newsletter contain news?

CHAPTER TWO

PLANNING TO PUBLISH

The world of writing and publishing is surrounded by myth and apocryphal tale. Of the Jeffrey Archer rags to riches story; of the poet starving in the attic; of the mysterious pencil trays in Roald Dahl's never cleaned garden hut; of the supreme irony of the Hitler diaries; and of those larger than life figures (and ex-figures) of publishing, Murdoch and Maxwell.

The mystique hides the simple truth. Writing and publishing is a task that requires dedication, hard work, an almost messianic zeal, a strategic mission statement, and a carefully drafted plan. From a two-page black and white stencilled local newsletter to a glossy, four-colour art paper production, the steps are broadly the same.

Step 1 - ESTABLISHING YOUR GOALS AND OBJECTIVES

How to set your goals

You should be able to summarise the purpose of your newsletter in a single twenty-word sentence. Newsletters are about a specific audience with a very small number of goals in mind. The more goals you aim for, the less impact you will achieve in each. Each goal statement should begin with a verb, and add to what you know about the identity of your readership.

Using your goals

You can use goals in planning for the publication. They can suggest a title for the publication, which stories to headline, what photos and graphics to use, the importance of the relationship between budget and image. There is always the lurking fear that a well-produced and glossy publication will attract criticisms of money wasted and too much spent on administrative costs. A shoddy newsletter may simply show the reader that you are a slipshod organisation. Good design and presentation will always enhance communication. However, the goal or purpose of the publication should provide the necessary guidance on the level of presentation.

- Have you got written goals and objectives for your newsletter?
- How do you measure if they've been achieved?
- Do you have an audience with a strong, common interest?
- Do you run a forward diary for future issues?
- When did you last visit your printer?

Chartown BULLETIN

PURPOSE	• to inform residents of the work of Chartown and Vosley Neighbourhood Council
GOALS	• increase awareness of work of Neighbourhood Council • establish Council as central to Chartown and Vosley community affairs • evaluate goals and objectives annually
OBJECTIVES	• improve circulation by 100 copies each issue • improve requests for inclusion of information by 10% each issue improve response to meetings of Neighbourhood by 10% each year

Purpose, goals, and objectives – your first building blocks for a successful publication

Some examples of goal statements:

- To persuade current supporters to recruit new supporters

- To raise regular funds from peripatetic supporters

- To inform professionals working in the field of current research into the disease

- To motivate donors to support our plans for change and progress

Chartown BULLETIN

Whoops

Thank you to all of you who let us know that you had received extra copies of our Chartown Resources Directory in May. We know it is annoying to get duplicate mailings. Please accept our sincere apologies.

The error was at the mailing house, and they assure us that it won't happen again. And, of course, they paid for the mistake. Please return your extra copies to us if you wish, and we'll pass them on to other interested groups.

Anyway, we hope you enjoyed our Resources Directory and are using it to find help when you need it.

Always remember how your readers and donors see your work

Chartown BULLETIN

Dear friends and supporters...

We hope you enjoy our Spring Newsletter. It comes with our best wishes and thanks for all you have enabled us to do for the Street Youth Project here in Chartown.

Rather than send individual letters, this is the Keystone Charity's way of saying thanks to each and every one of you. As you read the newsletter and project reports we hope you will share some of our pride in the achievements your support has made possible.

With that support, we are determined to tackle the scandal of bored youth on the streets of Chartown.

Use every chance to unify your target

If one of your goals is to impress funding bodies with the quality and worth of your medical research, then the purchase of more expensive paper, using photos and professionally produced graphics may well be worth the cost. Similarly, if yours is a subscription newsletter where the reader pays an annual membership fee, then they expect, and should get, a reasonable quality product.

For the smaller community group, however, it is the message about the activity and the news you provide that is vital, and the committed will want to see only the minimum expenditure to achieve this aim. One local charity distributes about 100 newsletters, and always asks for a stamped addressed envelope to be sent in by the reader for the next issue – plus any donations supporters can afford. Their supporter base has gently crept up from about sixty, and the only people who won't pay come from the statutory agencies! After much debate, they got their copies free.

Using objectives to reach your goals

From your goals, you should now develop some objectives for your publication. If the goals show where your newsletter is going, the objectives mark the places to be visited en-route. Objectives must contain *quantifiable* and *measurable* benefits, that can be reviewed and evaluated to judge your success.

Step 2 - IDENTIFY YOUR TARGET AUDIENCE

At first sight, identifying your audience is an easy task. Anyone and everyone with an actual or potential interest in your charity and its work could be interested in your publication. However, there are a variety of different interest groups associated with your work, each with special interests and concerns.

Usually a newsletter is launched with a specific target audience in mind, and as it succeeds in communicating with this group, other potential audiences are added to the distribution. At which point you should ask the questions – is the goal the same for each audience, and is this one publication the best medium for achieving it?

An increase in production and distribution numbers is often claimed as proof of success. It is, however, the response rates and the measurement of how well you are achieving your objectives and your goals that provide the best test.

Frequently Councillors and MPs are added to mailing lists so they can 'see our work come budget time'. These distributions are the fastest into the wastepaper bin. Few politicians will read anything not of direct interest to them – they're too busy and already swamped with paper. Far better a separate, more personal letter, with a brief overview of your work, written only to those who have a direct interest in what you are doing.

The most effective newsletters reach that specific audience which has a common interest, and will often identify the readership directly as part of the nameplate. You can then write directly to the action required from the reader. You will find that you get a good response almost every time.

Step 3 - PLANNING FOR PRODUCTION

There are a bewildering variety of steps in a production schedule, and it is highly dependent on the printing method. So there is no typically correct schedule. There are, however, some vital stages which should be noted.

Run a forward diary for issue themes

If you are producing a quarterly newsletter, select a basic theme for each issue to help plan the content. One publication date might be close to the annual conference. Another near the government benefit announcement which affects your clients and cashflow. These become natural themes for two of your issues. The third could be centred on a particular group of working projects. The fourth centre on new approaches to training or fundraising.

The beauty of this system is clear. It provides a focus, from which you can approach contributors well in advance to solicit the necessary contributions. Whilst some issues may be 'time related,' others are not. If you are overtaken by an emergency for the next issue, you will be able to postpone publication of prepared material to create space for the urgent news. Plus already have a 'focused' issue spare and already prepared for another time. It also helps writers if the focus is clear and planned, providing the necessary schedule and guidelines for them to prepare their contributions.

Print one, write one, plan one

You should, in effect, always have three issues in mind. One at proof, print or distribution stage. One at the writing stage. One being planned, with author contact and discussion under way.

The newsletter's name alone can target your readers most effectively

Here are some possible objectives for a hospice newsletter:

- To explain to our supporters why the search for a hospice site has taken so long so we spend less time in individual explanation to donors.

- To increase referrals to our centres from Health Visitors by 10 each month.

- To reduce poorly assessed referrals to our centres by clearly explaining our admission criteria.

- Your objectives should be reviewed at least annually. Each article in your newsletter should relate to an objective.

- If you are not measurably achieving at least some of your objectives each year, you should ask yourself if a newsletter is the correct medium for achieving your goals with this audience.

Chartown BULLETIN

Issue diary for 1995

There are six issues of the bulletin each year, and whilst some pages are set aside for news and diary items, there is always space for feature articles. Each issue will have a theme, so writers can focus on particular aspects of the same idea. Planned issues for next year are:

February 1995	Disability Survey: looking at arrangements for mobility in the High Street.
April 1995	Grants and Plans Special: council grants to projects announced, and charity spending plans.
June 1995	Childcare in Chartown: preparations and arrangements for the new school year.
August 1995	Summer Report: open air activities and leisure plans.
October 1995	Community Care in Chartown: is it working? Tell us what your experiences are.
December 1995	Christmas Cracker: all the Fayres and parties throughout the borough.

Thinking well ahead saves time, effort and personal crisis

Budgeting

Cost of course, is the ultimate nightmare. For most charities, the answer is usually simple – 'produce this for as little as possible, or perhaps a bit less!'. From the start divide potential costs into fixed costs and variable costs.

The variable costs are easiest to highlight, and tend to be those that relate to on the size and print run of the publication:

■ PAPER COSTS.
These depend on the quality of paper selected, the format and number of pages in the publication

■ PRINTING AND FOLDING COSTS.
Again the cost depends on size of publication, print run, and number of colours used

■ INSERTING, LABELLING AND POSTAGE.
Can you use volunteers, or a mailing house? Will you post or hand deliver? What is the weight of newsletter for posting?

The fixed costs are less obvious and less easy to quantify. The costs of your and your colleagues' time in information gathering, writing, photography, paste-up or DTP layout, proof reading etc.

As a rule of thumb, for short print runs (approximately 2,000 or less) pay most attention to the fixed costs. Be sure your objectives are realistic and that you are having have a direct and measurable impact in achieving them with your publication. Stop and consider the opportunity cost of your time.

Editors' Tales

"When my term as editor was over, I could finally look back at what I had achieved. Increased circulation, more responsive readership, new writers, regular columns -even getting the boss to approve the cost of colour printing.

Yet somehow each issue seemed to have got harder to produce. The pressure of deadlines was harsher, the decisions more difficult, the result somehow less satisfactory.

Determined to help the new editor, I told her two basic rules to help limit wasted effort. First, get organised. Draft a plan, and keep to it. Keep the same format, and don't change it for dramatic effect. Second, don't strive for perfection. Neither you nor the newsletter will ever be perfect – and there are many better things to do with the hours you waste trying to achieve it.

In truth, I had gone from being the reluctant amateur editor of a photocopied information sheet, to an enthusiastic press baron with a crusading message. I had been striving to achieve Fleet Street standards on no budget and hours of my own time.

Next time I edit a newsletter, perhaps I'll take my own advice!"

Request for an estimate

Here is a sample letter to be sent to a printer asking for a quote. You should approach at least three printers, possibly more, and not just those you've used before.

Dear_____

THE CHARTOWN BULLETIN

Please supply your estimate for printing a newsletter to the following specifications:

FORMAT: 4 page A4 newsletter, printed in black and one other colour throughout.

> A standard format for each issue.

MATERIALS: (a) 100 gsm smooth coated cartridge paper

(b) 85 gsm smooth coated cartridge paper

Please supply printed samples of the paper.

> Options for two different weights of paper.

QUANTITY: 2,000 and 250 run on

> The print quality and a price for a few additional copies to see if it's worth printing more.

ARTWORK: You will be supplied with camera ready artwork, with second colour marked on overlay. No bleeds in design, but allow for laying tints.

> Bleeds are where the printed area run off the edge of the paper. Half-tones are photographs. They need converting into dots before being printed.

DELIVERY: Packed in bundles of 250, delivered to one address in Chartown.

> If they are bundled in known quantities, it will make distribution easier.

Note this is a bi-monthly newsletter, and we require an estimate for six issues. Please advise of any early payment discount.

Quotations required by_____(date)

First issue to be distributed by_____(date)

> Good estimates always have specific breakdowns of all the relevant costs.

What else you could have been doing? Are the alternative uses of your time more effective in getting the message across?

As your print run grows longer, so the variable costs become more important. You can find wide variations in print quotations. There are many elements that go into the final figure for the production cost, and it is very important to break the quote down into specific expenditure items to truly compare costs. You must shop around and get estimates from several printers. When you do select one, work hard at maintaining a relationship with the printer – and take their advice! A good printer will frequently save you considerable time, effort and money.

Saving on postal costs

If you have a large subscriber (currently 5,000 plus) list you can cut mail costs through the Post Office Mailsort scheme. This requires you to pre-sort your addresses into postcode areas, which qualifies you for a discount. The Post Office give excellent guidance and assistance on how to use the scheme. But it can mean a lot of extra work for you and your volunteers – and should only really be considered if you can sort and print your address labels by Mailsort Code.

You might even consider posting from abroad according to International Postal Union agreements. Often cheaper, the drawbacks include extra time and cost of shipping the items to another country; the risk of losing some en route; and the questioning phone calls from supporters about the charity's new office in Budapest! But many commercial direct mail companies cut postage costs sharply this way.

Shop around, talk to other editors, and make an accurate estimate of your costs. But do try and work the budget up from your objectives. When you try and cram your objectives into a previously decided budget, quality, content and impact can all suffer.

Be very careful about 'obvious' cost savers, like sharing an envelope with three other items, or 'free' distribution through volunteer trees. If you have limited your goals to achieve the best impact, then why water it down by placing it in an envelope with three other items that seem, to the reader, to be all of equal (or negligible) importance?

If the newsletter is worth writing it's worth its own distribution. Response rates are consistently better when the newsletter arrives on time and on its own! Your budget must reflect these considerations.

Run a wall chart or diary system

Each issue is a project in its own right. Each step can be mapped on a time and development line. The chart opposite shows some vital steps.

Sample Editorial Planning Wallchart

Task	week 1	week 2	week 3	week 4	week 5
Gather information					
Cull copy from authors					
Plan photos, graphs, charts					
Edit/re-write copy					
Crop/select photos and charts					
Copy edit copy and visuals					
Proof-read copy and visuals					
Approve to printers or plate maker					
To mail house					

Step 4 - DO YOU LIKE THE RESULT?

This is probably the hardest step of all. You know all the shortcomings of your design and writing – you usually know what you would like to have seen produced. If cost was no object, or the money had been there for that extra colour, etc. The most important thing to remember is: 'your opinion doesn't count!'

The readers don't know what could have been – only what's there. You are writing for them not for yourself. So go and ask them what they think – there are plenty of hints for building reader response into your plan in chapter eight (page 73).

Now Decide...

■ Have you got written goals and objectives for your newsletter?

■ How do you measure if they've been achieved?

■ Do you have an audience with a strong, common interest?

■ Do you run a forward diary for future issues?

■ When did you last visit your printer?

CHAPTER THREE

WRITING SKILLS

Probably the best style of writing for newsletters would make your old English teacher's hair stand on end. The written word is the most important way to express your objectives and make an impact.

Photographs, design and graphics all have their place in getting the attention of the reader and highlighting the main points of your message. But only the written word can really cover all you want to say. You are not writing perfect prose.

Your writing style must get the information across to the reader during brief dips into the publication and before it is thrown away. Your newsletter will have to compete with a mass of other written material, as well as the usual noise and distraction of office or home. You should never forget that you are seeking success from a relatively weak medium, in a society that is spoon fed an easy diet of television and radio information.

Newsletter writing must be fast paced, informal, crisp, informative and simple. It should reflect the best and most natural, spoken language. When you speak to another person you tend to use simple language and easy images. Generally you are not over-concerned with the rules of grammar in such circumstances. So it is with the best newsletters.

> - Are you writing stories that readers want to read?
> - Do you use bullet points and checklists?
> - Have you included three short articles for each long one?
> - Are you writing simple, conversational English?
> - Got a stack of re-prints handy as a reserve?
> - Do you really need three columns?

> You are writing to be read, and to evoke a response from the reader. Before you read any more, stop and remind yourself of the life cycle of a newsletter:
>
> **It is dipped into for short periods of time**
>
> **It ends up in the waste paper bin**

The best writing starts with a planned focus, and an understanding of which objective you are writing to achieve. Consider the following checklist:

Writing survival skills

■ KEEP IT SHORT

The writing must match the nature of the publication. Sentences should be short – maximum 20 words. Paragraphs – maximum 6 sentences. And punctuation simple – usually limited to full stops, commas and the odd dash. This is a style sometimes called three dot journalism. It is also a tight discipline, which will help your reader.

Campaign Finance

Where the provision of information ceases to be seen by the law as educational and becomes primarily 'political' in purpose (and, as such, not charitable) is harder to explain, because it depends on the century-old accumulation of case-law and because the guidance from the Charity Commission is muddles. Political certainly does not just mean party-political, although campaigns that are *not* strongly divided on party lines (as in the Parents Against Tobacco example) probably benefit from greater freedom of interpretation. A (dangerous) simplification would be that anything directed towards changing the law is political. This is justified by one of those beautifully circular arguments at which the legal system excels. Charities must exist for the public benefit. The courts can only decide cases by the law as it stands.

How many times do you have to read these sentences before they really make sense?

The reader is always impatient, in a hurry and ready to be distracted. Tell them all you can, while you can.

Lord Chesterfield is claimed to have once written 'I apologise for sending you a five-page letter. I didn't have time to write you a one page letter'. He had a point. It is often easier to write 40 words when ten would do.

■ KEEP IT SIMPLE

Eliminate puffery, padding, jargon and politician speak. Even the most complex descriptions can be broken down into easily described stages.

'I remember a few years ago when my seven month old son had an intersusseption – a telescopic drawing in of the bowel on itself. Coming back from the hospital in the middle of the night, I explained it all as the doctor had told me, to the worried baby-sitting grandparents. In the morning facing the same baffling explanation to brother and sisters all under ten years old, I tucked a roll of my trouser leg and mimicked the action of the bowel. The understanding silence was broken only by Grandad....' So that's what you meant....'

Chartown BULLETIN

....the fact of the matter is success is measured by the event. If generated in a timely manner, from a period of some months advance planning, one can minimise errors in the majority of cases. By co-operating together whenever possible, substantial benefits can be achieved....

....Now that we have a greater degree of independence and a change of status and our major financial objectives have at least for the time being been overcome, I believe we can move into the new year with a degree of excitement and cautious optimism....

Can't see the point for the words!

Chartown BULLETIN

That is why Petra's picture is here, not mine. To remind me – and you, if you need reminding – that she is who matters. The Keystone Charity operates only two projects. For the remainder, we are one step removed, as we fund others. It is easy to be so removed that I forgot the people we exist to serve – like Petra, her family and her friends.

Articles have impact when they're short and real

We all have our pet hate pompous words and phrases. Why *implement*, when you can *do*? Is the word *utilise* of any *use* at all? How many times have you heard a politician say: *the fact of the matter is?* What does it mean – either there is a fact or there isn't! These phrases have a habit of spawning new variants as well. A government minister recently answered a parliamentary question starting: 'with all due respect, the facts of the matter are quite clear'. Oh no they're not!

Please understand how difficult this can be – it is debunking the habits of a lifetime. Since we learned to write our name at school, through 11+ or assessment, school essays, college exams and office memoranda, we are encouraged to write to impress the reader. We want to show them not only our grasp of the subject matter, but also our knowledge of the jargon, and the floridity and fluidity of our linguistic ability.

Please forget it all. Write to express your thoughts in the quickest and simplest way you can. You will not get hundreds of letters from grateful readers. In fact, few people will notice all of this hard work. But more will read on towards the end of articles and turn over to other pages.

■ KEEP IT SPECIFIC

Use dates, times, numbers, places. Do not use general words and phrases. Where possible, avoid abstract concepts in favour of facts and figures. Remember it is only desperate, urgent, or unique if you can prove it. Your reader wants the quickest, clearest information.

Do not write: 'A large number of supporters attended....'

But rather: 'Over 400 Under Fives attended the Fun Day on 15th June....'

■ BEWARE SPELL CHECK

It is easy to create a howler, this is simply shown by example:

The political newsletter that profiled Chairman of the Conservative Party ' Norman Teapot' (Tebbitt);

The parish magazine that wrote of 'The Tower of Babble' (Babel)

■ USE LISTS AND BULLET POINTS

Readers love lists and you can highlight key points with bullet points.

- Develop different symbols – be consistent with regular features.

- Don't number unless you wish to indicate priorities.

- Research shows lists and bullet points greatly improve retention

- It makes you identify key points and write them down yourself.

■ USE STRONG VERBS AND ACTIVE VOICE

Drive the reader on, and keep the writing on the move. Strong verbs link to the senses or the emotions and fit easily with other strong words. Weak verbs are more abstract and link to longer adverbs. Address the reader as 'you' – and tell them how we will solve the problem, (and not the passive, 'the problem will be solved by').

■ USE FAMILIAR LANGUAGE

You can and should begin sentences with and, but, because, so, it. You shouldn't worry about using contractions, they can't hurt and won't delay the reader at all.

■ LOOK OUT FOR WORDS THAT AREN'T NEEDED

A round circle; 48cm in **length**; this **moment** in time etc! The best and least expensive piece of an editor's equipment is the red pencil. Use it on every paragraph.

SYMPTOMS

 Fever/Vomiting

 Severe headache

 Neck stiffness and joint pains

 Dislike of bright lights

 Drowsiness, coma

 Rash

Babies may also suffer:
- Swelling of the fontanelle (soft spot on the forehead)
- Blotchy or pale skin
- Staring expression
- Fretfulness
- Shrill or moaning cry especially when handles
- Rash - initially tiny red spots rapidly developing into large purple or red bruises which could appear anywhere on the body

These symptoms may not appear all at the same time.

Bullet points highlight the vital information

■ BE AWARE OF SEXIST AND RACIST LANGUAGE

Always a very sore point with much of the charity world. Such bias often creeps in subconsciously, there are many classic examples:

'Chief Executive, Mr Brown and his secretary, Gwyneth...'

'A homosexual man with AIDS...'

'A non-drinking Irish policeman...'

'The charity has a female Director...'

Don't forget:

■ Your opinion doesn't count!

■ Think of the reader.

Essentially you must be sure that the language you use is sensitive to the interest of your readership. At the nub of this problem is the aim to communicate, not upset or distract.

For some charities the relative use of 'he' or 'she', 'Chairman' 'Chairperson' or 'Chair' and other similar terms is a big issue. But the penalties for calling one of your county ladies who raises large sums for your cause 'Ms' may be just as severe!

What's news?

So now we have a focus, and guidelines for appropriate writing. What material is best put into the articles?

Reader research comes up time after time with NEWS as the context readers most look for. This is followed by:

Chartown BULLETIN

Staff Memo

Before you hand any piece of writing to the editor – THINK!

How does this piece help us achieve our goal?

Can you link your writing to a goal or objective of the newsletter?

■ Feature articles, full of information

■ Examples of the charity's people and work

■ Calendars and events diaries

■ Columns: special contributions by people whose views may be of interest

Clearly the order of importance will affect the layout. First comes the news – on the most-read first and last pages or on the outside covers. In priced newsletters, the item that makes most people renew their subscriptions is the news.

So what is news? News is events, developments, decisions that affect the reader, outcomes of meetings, new policy decisions, changes in government strategy, fundraising successes and the progress of campaigns.

What isn't news?

News is not personal news about employees, their marriages, their birthdays, and so on. Not only does this not truly interest your readers, but if circulation widens it simply excludes others who may not know the characters involved. And remember, it is your readers who will say 'Do I care about this ?' You must pick topics that your readers will want to learn about.

Yes, you cry, what about the day when there is no real news? Then cheat – use bigger photographs, and adapt your most interesting feature articles to the front page. It is easier to get away with this in a newsletter than a newspaper. Newsletters are less frequent and can use their common interest base to push a suitable feature story.

For newspapers, when the reader sees the various different stories on the front pages of different papers in the newsagent, it's obviously a no news day. Your newsletter is usually read by someone who has a basic interest in the subject anyway, and is more open to attraction by the writing.

Where to start?

There is a set formula used worldwide by journalists for a basic style of writing. After the first few times you use it, habit takes over and it all gets easier.

The first paragraphs need the 5W's – WHO, WHAT, WHY, WHEN and WHERE – but not necessarily in that order.

Who was involved – Trevor Sharp and Keystone Charity

What happened – condemned government report

Where did it happen – at the conference

When did it happen – following the Minister's statement

Why did it happen – because the Minister alleged the charity had used government money improperly

The first paragraph should be kept as short as possible. It is the hook that gets the reader to read on. Or the basic facts for the reader who only scans the publication. The remainder of the story rolls on like a pyramid. Ideally, each section should only be one paragraph. The longer the article, the fewer people will read to the end.

> ## *Chartown* BULLETIN
>
> ### Two years wait for ambulance
> Early one Sunday morning, Rita Cox collapsed while giving out hymn books in St. Phillips Church. Twenty two minutes after the 999 call was made an ambulance arrived having come all the way from Volsey. All attempts to resuscitate Rita failed.
>
> Whenever Chartown residents dial 999 the ambulance must come from Volsey, five and a half miles away, at the end of a busy dual carriageway often jammed with traffic. Yet Chartown is a bigger place, with more residents, and growing faster.
>
> The Health Authority tell us that a new ambulance station will be built in Chartown in 1996. How many more stories like Rita's will there be in the next two years?

A simple local news story

> ## *Chartown* BULLETIN
>
> ### Sharp damns report on abuse of funds
> At the Keystone Charity's Annual Conference Trevor Sharp angrily condemned the recent government report alleging poor money management. Responding to the Minister's accusations of improper use of government funds, Sharp challenged the author to produce the evidence of abuse. "We have nothing to hide" he declared, as he opened yesterday's proceedings at Church House.
>
> The Buttolph Report was published three weeks ago and may threaten continued government support for Keystone's local Project. This was the subject of the first debate at the conference. It attracted vocal support from the thirty families who use the centre, and are concerned that its services will be withdrawn.
>
> The Keystone Charity has worked in Chartown for more than ten years and is well known throughout the local community.

Using the 5Ws for simple presentation

This formula was developed for typesetting in newspaper production. If the crucial information sits at the top of the story, then the typesetter didn't need permission to re-write if the article was too long for copyfitting – the story's later paragraphs could be cut to fit the page.

The formula still supplies compact, succinct news presentation that can be seen in a host of papers and magazines every day. It also helps you edit easily, and avoids too much waffle and deathless prose; no-one can risk saving the clever stuff until the last couple of lines! Remember, your writing will be skim read by busy people – you must be certain they can pick up the gist of your story swiftly.

A typical structure may be:

1st section
CRUCIAL INFORMATION (5W'S)

2nd section
MORE DETAIL

3rd section
BACKGROUND INFORMATION

4th section
FUTURE OPTIONS

5th section
ACTION AND CONSEQUENCES

Chartown BULLETIN

Peter gets in first

Peter Herbert was in a hurry to get home. Tuesday was the best day for television and it had been a long, hard day at the shops. He dashed down the street and in through the front door with his mum's keys. But he left mum outside and could not manage the latch. He was locked in and she was locked out.

Jane went straight to the Keystone Project in the Square. She knew she would find someone to help her, a working telephone to summon others if required. The project has received over ten thousand general enquiries about estate matters during the past two years. It has helped many in distress when council offices are simply too far away. With Keystone ladders and caretakers help, Jane was soon back in her flat.

And Peter? Whilst he could not open the door, he knew how to turn on the television – and miss none of his programme.

Sandwich the facts of the story between personal experience

Presenting your best features

Features are useful to both inform and entertain readers, and also to break up longer news information. Tests show that most readers prefer two short stories to one long one. You can also use features to tempt readers inside your newsletter – a brief front page story with 'for more on this see inside'. Long biographical detail can be signposted that way, or displayed through a sidebar alongside the main story.

You can use a greater variety of writing styles in presenting features – there are five that are regularly used, and provide a wide scope for presenting most feature pieces.

■ THE WALL STREET DIAMOND OR WSJ TECHNIQUE

Present the story as a personal experience, expand to explain the basic facts, then return to the specific experience or example at the end.

Suppose you're writing about the introduction of a new affinity card for your charity. Start with the specifics; one of your supporters whose bank offered her the card. Then branch out; explain the number of cards issued, how the scheme works, its development, how the charity hopes it will be used and what it will be worth in fundraising terms. Then finish with the specifics again – Joan is happy shopping with her card, knowing she is being a donor at the same time!

■ EXTENDED DIALOGUE

People read quotes. It is the reading equivalent of eavesdropping. To present a feature as 'We talked to people to get their views...' After the introducing paragraph is also effective. You don't need names, but is excellent for putting across honest opinion on difficult topics. Could be used for listing comments from people upset by situations – the imposition of VAT on fuel; changing a logo or charity name etc.

■ FIRST PERSON

Remember that a newsletter is more personal in its approach than a newspaper or magazine. Journalists are brainwashed to always use the third person – but you musn't overuse the first person either. It is an excellent way of writing about an emotional or tense situation, expressing character, bravery and generating empathy.

But do use this technique sparingly – once per issue or even every other issue, and only one article in each issue. Also only use 'I' the minimum number of times; once, perhaps, per paragraph. This is a proven technique that loses its effect if used too often. Its very success depends on standing out as being different from the rest of the writing.

■ THE INTERVIEW

Probably the most popular format with readers- particularly if you can get in touch with celebrity or well known figure. It can also help get a personal insight into what may be a distant figure, such as your new Patron. But the figure should be of interest – and that's where many of us fall down-running out of genuinely interesting figures quite quickly.

Sometimes the interview is best adapted into a column format – such as *A Day in the Life of* or *My most difficult day* which can take both well known figures and those who may simply work in areas most of us know little about.

■ QUESTION AND ANSWER FORMAT

An easy way out if you are in a hurry – and a useful way of presenting a summary of facts and information. List the four or five main questions people may have about this particular change or new project – the key questions. This also ensures that all the essential information reaches a wide audience, and is a clear and helpful way to present detailed or technical information.

Keep an ideas file

Whichever technique you choose, it's certain there are examples all around you in everything you read. So start an ideas file today. Clip out feature articles that interest you and try and adapt the ideas for your publication. Having an ideas file has saved many an editor in filling their pages on a murky Friday in February.

Or try asking the readers. What are the areas of the charity's work they'd most like to hear about?

In summary, when writing for your newsletter be aware of style changes for news or features; don't waffle or over punctuate; keep it short; keep it simple; be aware of your readers – and if in doubt, leave it out! When all is said and done, your opinion is the least important of all – it is the readers' reaction that counts!

Diary notes and dates

There are other areas of content worth considering for all newsletters.

My Stay in Hospital
by "The Bionic Woman" (Zahra)

Hi kids of Chettle Court!

I'll tell you about my stay in the Whittington Hospital. The reason I am in hospital is that I got run over at the top of Ferme Park Road on the 29th December. I was walking along the road and then I went to cross the road and I was hit by a car, but I can't remember exactly what happened. I broke my pelvis in two places, my shoulder, and had two blood clots in my head. I was taken to the Royal London Hospital by helicopter. I was airlifted but I cannot remember anything about it. My brother was the first person I remember seeing by my bed. I stayed at this hospital for about two weeks then I was taken to the Whittington Hospital

Today is Monday the 31st January and I am lying in my bed and the time is 1:15pm. I am going to tell you a bit about the way the hospital is run and how I feel.

Used well, a first person story makes the reader think hard

Hi my name's Belinda Linden and as Nurse Advisor at the British Heart Foundation, I give cardiac advice and information to heart patients and their carers, as well as the professionals.

Here's a few of the most commonly asked questions; in future issues I'll be making other selections.

But if there is something that is particularly worrying you, or about which you need more information, just get in touch.

Q I'm a non-smoking female, about 5 foot 4 inches tall, with a weight of 8st 10lbs. I pick food between meals and exercise regularly as I am worried about my weight. Should I lose weight to protect my heart?

A It appears from your low body weight and non-smoking that your risk of heart disease is quite small and you shouldn't try to lose any further weight, Don't worry about increased body fat in the lower part of your body, as this is thought by many doctors to be less harmful than having more weight at the top of your body.

An excellent way to communicate basic factual information

Chartown BULLETIN

Diary
June – July 1995

Sun 5th June Street Youth Project disco,
7.30–10.30pm, St. Phillips Church
Hall, Marsten Street Entrance
£1.25.

Mon 6th June Chess Club, 7.00–9.30pm, Volsey
Neighbourhood Centre, Norton
Towers.

Wed 8th June Auditions for 'Harlequinade'
8.00pm, Volsey Neighbourhood
Centre, Norton Towers.

Sat 11th June Tea Dance, 5.00–8.00pm, St.
Phillips Church Hall, Marsten
Street.

Sun 12th June Keystone Fundraising Sponsored
Walk, 2.00pm, commencing
Keystone Project Building,
Reading Street.

Mon 13th June School Sports Day, 1.30pm, Volsey
Junior School (cancelled if wet).

Mon 20th June Street Youth Project Carnival,
starting 6.30pm, Keystone Project
Building, Reading Street

*What's happening in your area is
important news*

SOMEWHERE TO RUN?
By Nick Hardwick, Director of Centrepoint

One of the saddest documents at Centrepoint is the Missing Persons File – page after page of letters and photos sent to us by parents, relatives and friends desperately searching for a young person who has run away from home. However, for each young person who has someone desperately looking for them, there are dozens of others who have no one who cares where they are.

We define runaways as young people who cannot legally live away from home. In most cases, this means children under the age of sixteen. We see between 10 and 15 underage runaways every month, some as young as thirteen. Very few of these have left a loving parental home after a minor argument. Young people like that go home quite quickly once they find out how bad life is on the streets.

Our experience is that young people do not usually run away – and stay away – unless there is something seriously wrong. Most of the runaways we see have run away from Children's Homes.

*Directors' Columns can be used very
effec-tively to direct readers to
particular problems*

Formal advertising is dealt with in a chapter nine (page 81). But for many smaller groups the inclusion of small ads, or a bulletin board allows readers to swap second hand equipment or aids for sufferers.

Surveys show that the classified pages are often the most highly read. The next most highly read are the calendar or forthcoming events and activities pages. This should be included for all charity newsletters as this is real news for most of the readership.

Fundraising events, meetings, rallies, lobbying activities – all have their place, and can usefully inform your readers of the charity's activities each month or quarter. Do be careful with your forward diary of events if you only publish quarterly. Some of those dates may be four months away when you get the information. And have a nasty habit of changing in that time.

Do look carefully at the layout of your calendar to be sure that the basic information the reader needs can be picked off one line. Don't make them dodge back to another spot for information or details such as the day of the week, the venue or whatever. The presentation should allow the information to be easily scanned and absorbed. The calendar should be on the same page of each edition. Calendars are pointers that readers will look for, and you must not shift them from page to page.

In a standard four page A4 newsletter most people will read the page order 1-4-3-2. The news items should go on either front or back page. Many editors put their calendar news on the back page for this reason.

Columns and comment

Another regular feature is columns – sketch columns, comment columns, and often either the Director's or Chief Executive's column, plus an Editor's column for you to say what you want (but see below). Used properly, these can be a welcome part of each issue. They can include:

- The News in Brief type approach, which can summarise very effectively a wide range of activities.

- A People Column reviewing joiners, leavers and retiring staff and volunteers;

- A Readers' Comments or Letters Page.

- A Guest Column.

In many charity newsletters, the Director's column is an established and regular feature. In others, the Editor's Column fills that regular slot. In mercifully few, you can be unlucky enough to get both. This is really a technique copied from newspapers and magazines, where editorial is the heart of the message.

■ DIRECTORS WRITE REALLY BORING STUFF!

If your Director's Column is tedious, then edit it as ruthlessly as any other piece of the content. Give it an interesting headline or sub-headings. If all else fails, don't give it a headline at all, and put it in the lower half of page 2 (remember the reading order 1-4-3-2!).

The point is that Directors' Columns are not inevitable or always required. Most are over long – editors hesitate before pruning the boss too sharply – and often long winded. They betray too easily the question the writer asks before they start to write – now what shall we put in the newsletter this time?

■ CONTENTS COLUMN

A contents column will be needed for publications more than six pages long, this will require numbered pages throughout the newsletter.

The contents column should be placed regularly in the same position. It is a form of news for the reader, and is usually scanned by all who dip into the publication to select their order of reading. Contents columns might contain a brief outline of each article to explain a little more fully what each piece is about. Another useful idea is to print a small photo alongside each article title, as an attention grabber and a hint as to content.

The Director's Column

Try asking yourself the following questions:

- Do you – or the boss – have excellent writing skills?
- Is what you write only coverable in a comment or opinion column – or is it really news?
- Would either column be strengthened if they appeared irregularly – when there is something very important to say?
- Why do you think newspaper columnists are highly paid for what they do?
- Do you write other parts of the publication? Do you really need to write more?
- Do the columns merely fill available space rather than improve the content?

Think this through. Does it make sense to drop the regular columns? Or spread the burden of writing them ? Can you invite outside opinions, or guest editorials? Can you focus the columns more effectively that way?

Three different approaches to listing contents

Now Decide...

- Are you writing stories that readers **want** to read?

- Do you use bullet points and checklists?

- Have you included three short articles for each long one?

- Are you writing simple, conversational English?

- Got a stack of re-prints handy as a reserve?

- Do you really need three columns?

■ REPRINTING OUTSIDE MATERIAL

A final thought that has been a life-saver to many a busy editor short of material for the next issue. From today start scouring all the newspapers, magazines and newsletters that you read for articles that may be of interest to your readers. When you find one, clip it out and write to the publishers, asking permission to reprint it in your limited circulation newsletter – offering full credit to the original source. Rarely will permission be refused, and you will start to build a file of back-up material to use in your newsletter that is quickly available as and when you need it, of known quality, and interesting.

CHAPTER FOUR

WHAT MAKES A GOOD EDITOR ?

Almost all charity newsletters are produced by employees as only one part of their job, or by a volunteer as a part-time work. Whether you are an employee or a volunteer, the art of getting the editing right is all about communication with others. The writers, the printers, the readers, and all those you'd like to persuade to be readers.

The key is planning effectively and working to that production plan – as discussed in Chapter 2 'PLANNING TO PUBLISH'. You should aim to get approximately one and a half times as much material as you need for each issue, and edit it utterly ruthlessly.

Which leads neatly to the issue of editorial freedom. In most cases the organisation that publishes the newsletter expects some benefit or return for itself. And the editor's job is to achieve that benefit.

- ■ What do you like about being an editor?
- ■ Writing most of the newsletter yourself?
- ■ How do you motivate/reward your writers?
- ■ Got an information pack for your contributors?
- ■ When do you undertake your annual review of the newsletter?

First make sure there is an agreed purpose, and a method of monitoring if it is being achieved.

Second, ensure that only one person is responsible for final decisions on length and content (the editor).

Third, if you have a supervisor or committee to help you with the work, they should agree these points before you really start.

Got enough writers?

A frequent problem is recruiting enough writers to produce the material. Otherwise there's nothing for you to edit. When first starting out, editors seem to spend a lot of time writing the articles to go in their newsletter. Like many other elements in producing the newsletter, a planned long term approach will produce writers if you tackle it correctly and early on. There are two important strategies you must put in place – a planned approach, and information pack guiding writers to a your requirements.

■ STEP ONE

Run an editorial diary, giving each issue a focus, and start the planning as early as possible.

Editors' Tales

"Of course the charity and its director own the newsletter, but I really work for the donors and supporters of our work. I'm constantly surprised at how many get in touch, asking for information, follow-ups on particular stories, or just questions about the work.

And they expect honesty. If a project goes wrong and mistakes are made, they want to know. And it's part of my job to tell them. It's their money and their belief in what we do that keeps us going. But sometimes, them upstairs would like figures a little more massaged, and presentationally more correct.

Sometimes you're stuck between the devil and the deep blue sea. Recently, our charity made a thumping great loss on the sale of a holiday hotel it had bought only 4 years ago. Trade magazines were full of the fall in hotel values, the local press and radio were openly speculating on the figures. When researching my article for the newsletter, the hotel manager gave me the estate agent's estimate, and the original purchase price.

The Project Director wrote to all the hotel employees banning them from talking to the press, warning them that disclosure was a serious disciplinary offence. He then dropped in to see me, hoping that the figures would not be included in the article, as it might embarrass the organisation.

My article 'The end of an era', brought dozens of letters from readers all over the country. Some fondly remembered holidays in the hotel, others running events to raise funds to send clients there.

Only one mentioned the figures. The article had explained with great care why the decision had been taken, which was in part to fit better with clients' expectations of their leisure time.

The Project Director was furious – and spent much time and many meetings explaining the decision. But shouldn't he have done that in the first place? Charities make decisions that involve financial loss every day. Clear, simple, and honest explanation usually works best. Good editors take readers and the truth very seriously."

■ STEP TWO

Recruit to that diary. Every visit you make, function you attend, other newspaper or newsletters you read, are sources of potential writers. If you attend too many meetings an ideal method of reducing invitations is to ask for contributions at each one – they'll soon stop inviting you to those meetings where your presence isn't vital! More seriously, do talk to everyone you meet about the importance of having a wide range of contributions for the newsletter.

■ STEP THREE

Having chatted, follow up with a formal invitation to write the article. Include sample copies of past newsletters and be clear about the deadlines. Step three (b) is, of course, the follow up telephone call and letter to check it's all really happening!

■ STEP FOUR

This step is probably the most important. You must reward the writer for doing the piece. Praise works wonders. Certificates, coffee mugs, tee-shirts, badges, even little plaques can all be displayed that to show this person is a writer. Similarly by-lines or short biographies in the newsletter, and the chance to be an associate editor, if, say, five articles are submitted to deadline. The vital thing to remember is that just as with donors, although initial recruitment can be time consuming and expensive, most people are good for more than one contribution.

There is other bait you can use. Many people just like the idea of having something published, and building a reputation as a writer. Here s a chance for them to build a portfolio of work, and retain the chance to re-use it after its first publication in your newsletter.

Some groups hold a newsletter annual lunch or meeting just for newsletter contributors. This could include a tour of magazine or newspaper offices. The important thing to remember is to keep the relationship with any potential writers a two way activity, so there's something clearly in it for them as well.

Don't write, just report

Others may not wish to write directly, but may be willing to report – feed you with ideas and stories that may be of interest for the newsletter from their department or section. This is particularly useful for multiple-site organisations, where office correspondents may keep the editor in touch with local events and news.

This does not invalidate having visitors writing their impressions of that local project as well. In fact it makes the whole exercise much more interesting! Because the newsletter must be lively and not just push a 'party line' continuously. Healthy debate must come off its pages sometimes.

The second important point is to have a common pack of information for all potential contributions. These are simple should only be brief but cover the following:

- Purpose, goals and objectives of the publication
- Summary information about the readership
- A reporters' sheet – to be photocopied – setting out a style for reporters so all their reports come to you in the same format. Usually, but not exclusively in the 5W's layout.
- An editor's sheet – covering hints on consistency of writing – form for names, writing times, use of abbreviations and making it clear all writing will be edited by you.

This is something both editors and writers get very worried about. Simply edit everything as a matter of routine – it will always improve the sharpness of the point being made.

The different tasks

Do remember however that copy editing and proof reading are two distinct and separate tasks. When copy editing, check and correct the writing –

Chartown Bulletin style sheet

Name:	Full name when first mentioned, thereafter common name used etc. No degrees or letters after name.
	Department or position if vital to the story.
Numerals:	Words in body copy, numerals in headlines, unless combinations (5 million) more easily understood.
	In series use all numerals, 7, 8, 9. and 14
Symbols:	Words in body copy and headlines except £. In tables use symbols at top of column only.
Times/dates:	Twelve hour clock, numerals + AM/PM ie 11-00 am.
	Numeral only plus written month and full year (if required) 7 February 1994.
Abbreviations:	Standard address format acceptable (Glos) in address lists; spell in full (Gloucestershire) in text.
Headlines:	Sentence structure; capital letters for words according to normal use. Max fifteen words.
Spelling:	Beware US based spellcheck software. Crosscheck with standard English dictionary.
Mode of address:	Don't use Mr. Mrs. Ms. Titles if relevant to story in full first use, thereafter standard abbreviation – Councillor Valerie Groves – Cllr Groves
Capital letters:	Official titles (Mayor), departments (Housing Benefit), as required by grammar.
Story presentation:	Double spaced typewritten on one side of paper, similar layout on disk. Staple separate sheet with name, address, contact number
Reporter format:	If not written as article, name, address, contact number at top of sheet, then five paragraphs, who, what, why, when, where.
Deadlines:	Received in office by last day of February, May, August, November each year.
	Handwritten items, faxes, tape or answerphone stories ignored!

including spelling, punctuation and grammar, check for sentences that don't make sense, and conformity to the editor's sheet.

Proof reading examines final copy for errors, omissions and layout, accuracy on the page – missed commas and full stops and similar keyboard problems. It is very hard to proof read or copy edit your own writing. It's much easier to read someone else's. You correct what is on the page, not what you remember writing. It is always worth getting a colleague who hasn't been involved to date to check proofs for you.

Management review

The editor must set aside the time for the managerial tasks. Newsletters

☐ ☐

Writing Exercise: Keeping it Simple

Here are three samples of newsletter writing that need editing. You can test your editorial skills by making them shorter, punchier, and more interesting.

■ *DIRECTOR'S COLUMN*

As I approach ten years as Director, it seems a good time to take stock of the growth and development of this organisation, that is now the cornerstone of so many carers lives. It has not always been smooth progress, and I suspect that you, like me, are stronger and wiser than we were. Certainly, the commitment of our volunteers and supporters has never been in any doubt. My postbag bears testimony to the excellent levels of skills and experience that is the hallmark of our helpers. I look forward, with some degree of humility, to the achievements of the next ten years. Which, like the last ten , will be thanks to you and your efforts.

Would this be better?

THANK YOU!

The thank you letters I get from clients remind me constantly of your work. You, the volunteers, your dedication and skill, have built our reputation for excellent work. With your help, our work will continue to prosper.

■ *STAFF WIN AWARD*

The Chartown Charity employees are a dedicated, hardworking, bunch, as many of you know. They provide an excellent service to clients, and cope with all sorts of extraordinary crisis en route. Now they're officially champions, however. At a ceremony in the Town Hall, they received the highest award in the council's 'Quality comes first' annual event. The competition looked at customer service, handling enquiries, prompt response to correspondence, excellence in handling telephone calls. and value for money.

Would this be better?

QUALITY COMES FIRST!

Our staff have won the Council's annual award for excellence in customer service. They were top in:
- *Handling enquiries*
- *Swift response to letters and phone calls*
- *Value for money.*

But we knew that....didn't we! Well done!

■ *BUS PASS BENEFITS*

So many of you have asked for our pamphlet 'Getting the best from your bus pass', that we've had to re-print it. This pamphlet was written on the understanding that it would provide a simple guide to the benefits available to the elderly, disabled and families in our town. It is our hope that new copies of the pamphlet will be available by the first of next month. Your take up of this offer has proved to be of great significance to the organisation, and we would like to express our gratitude that you clearly value our service.

Would this be better?

REQUEST STOP!

So many of you have written for copies of our practical guide to of 'Getting the best from your bus pass', that we have run out. We're reprinting and copies will be available on the 1st August. Come and get it then, and plan your cheap summer days out!

Shorten that word

The aim of newsletter writing is to get the message to the reader quickly and simply. Here's a sample list of words we all use regularly when writing – and their easy, short alternatives. Make up your own full list, and stick it on the wall next to your keyboard.

ACCOMPLISH .... do	ELIMINATE .... cut
ACQUIRE ....get	ENCOUNTER .... meet
ADVANTAGEOUS .... helpful	EVIDENT .... clear
ASSISTANCE .... help	EXPERTISE .... skill
BE IN COMMUNICATION WITH .... say, write	FACILITATE .... help
BE IMPLEMENTED BY ....done	FINAL .... last
BEST INDICATION .... sign	FORFEIT ....lose
BEING INFORMED BY. .... told	FOR THE PURPOSE OF .... because
CONSEQUENTLY .... so	HOWEVER .... but
CONTAINS .... has	HAS THE RESULT .... ends
CONTRIBUTE .... give	HAS INSUFFICIENT.... .... not enough
CONCERNING .... about	HAS INDICATED THAT... .... shown
DEMONSTRATE .... show	IMMEDIATELY .... now
DISCONTINUE .... stop	IN ACCORDANCE WITH .... by
DO NOT .... don't	IN ADDITION .... plus
DUE TO THE FACT .... since	IN ORDER THAT .... so
JAM TOGETHER .... join	REQUIREMENT .... need
JAM PACKED ....packed	RESIDE ....live
JOKER IN THE PACK .... odd one out	RETAIN .... keep
JUST REACHED OUR GOAL .... made it	RESIDUAL ....left
LEGISLATION .... Law	SIMILAR TO .... like
LIMITED NUMBER ....few	STATE OF THE ART .... latest
LOCATE ....find	SUBSEQUENTLY .... after
LOCATION ....place	SUFFICIENT .... enough
MAGNITUDE .... size	TERMINATE .... stop
MINIMISE .... reduce	THEREFORE .... so
MODIFY .... change	TIMELY MANNER .... prompt
MOST OF THE TIME .... usually	THEATRICAL .... dramatic
NO LATER THAN .... by	UTILISE .... use
NOTIFY .... tell	UNDER WAY .... moving
NUMEROUS .... many	UNITARY .... single
NECESSITY .... need	UNIFORM MANNER .... same
OBSERVE ....see	VALUE .... cost
OBTAIN ....get	VERBATIM ....exact
OPTIMUM .... best	VIABLE .... practical
OPTION ....choice	VIRTUOUS ....good
POINT IN TIME .... now	WHENEVER .... when
PREPARED .... ready	WHEREAS .... since
PRIOR TO ....before	WITH REFERENCE TO .... about
PROVIDED THAT .... if	WITH THE EXCEPTION OF .... except

are like any small business, that can fail for lack of planning and control. So here are some points to consider for regular review:

- Purpose, goals, objectives – are they still the same ?

- Are they being achieved?

- Encouraging writers and reporters – thank them, discuss article ideas with them

- Recruiting new writers – always be on the hunt, getting one new writer per issue?

- Training – for yourself and for your established contributors

- Readership and audience surveys – formal and informal mechanisms for communication and feedback

- Checking technology changes in DTP – look at what other groups are using

- Evaluation of benefit to the publishing organisation – and whether you are achieving your goals? How do others see the achievement?

- Suggestions for new content – scan other newsletters for fresh ideas

- Checking sub-editing skills – give the last issue to another editor for comment!

Sub-editing

Sub-editing is a vital part of the editor's role. Have you placed material in the right order – analysing the most effective order of priority for the information? Where it is placed in the publication?

How does the news value of each item match with the image and purpose of the newsletter? How good are the subheadings and quotations used – do they follow a logical sequence and allow readers to skip paragraphs if necessary?

Have you used photos, diagrams and graphic devices, and do these reinforce or distract from the main message?

In all of this, you shouldn't forget your own rewards. Hopefully you'll get a sense of doing a worthwhile job, and a degree of creative satisfaction from your work. The job of editing a newsletter will mean you will learn new skills, and perhaps find new job opportunities. Above all, in the charity world, you will be part of the vital information network that gets your campaign message across. You will help keep your volunteers enthused and committed, and your donors giving money to your cause.

Now Decide...

- Writing most of the newsletter yourself?

- How do you motivate/reward your writers?

- Got an information pack for your contributors?

- When do you undertake your annual review of the newsletter?

- What do you *like* about being an editor?

CHAPTER FIVE

PERKING UP YOUR PAGES, SELLING THE STORY

Of all the adages in newsletter lore, one is most important - that readers will read what they want to read, not what they ought to read.

It is the prime duty of the editor to ensure that the newsletter is lively, interesting – and grabs the reader's attention every time. The common interest audience is often seen as not needing the same treatment as a broader readership – but the assumption that supporters will read anyway is a false one.

Two items usually attract readers to particular pages or particular stories. Firstly, if there is a photograph or drawing. Secondly if it has an interesting or attention grabbing headline. These are the places where the eye goes to first when scanning the page. If you can afford the extra costs, photos are a valuable addition to your pages.

Good photographs are worthwhile – *but they must be good.* Too often newsletters are full of pictures of buildings, fundraising groups waving at some vague point to the left of the photographer, grip and grins (cheque handovers!), posed pictures of this or that committee at work, or passport booth snapshots of new staff – usually on a bad day!

Guidelines for photographers

A few simple guidelines for photographers would help, as with the editor's sheet for writers.

■ BLACK AND WHITE PHOTOGRAPHS

These are best for black and white and two-colour newsletters. Colour works better for four colour reproduction. The printing of colour photos in black and white usually means loss of definition, shade and contrast. For two-colour printing, the photographs will always reproduce sharper when they are printed in black and white than in the second colour.

- ■ Is your most important story on the front page?
- ■ Do you use the best photograph on the front page?
- ■ Got a tips sheet and film for your photographers?
- ■ Are your headlines lively and interesting?
- ■ Use a lot of subheadings on the page?
- ■ Do you vary how the articles finish?
- ■ How expensive does the newsletter look?

A striking image – or a background to skip?

VOLUME 38 No. 4 WINTER 1992

T A L K I N G
SENSE

THE MAGAZINE OF SENSE, THE NATIONAL DEAF-BLIND AND RUBELLA ASSOCIATION

IN THIS ISSUE	Speaking Sense unto power	Care or Chaos	In Depth
	Sense at work at the party conferences *page 3*	Challenging the politicians on Community Care *page 4*	Reports from Sense's 1992 Weekend Away *pages 10-21*

People speak louder than buildings

The best pictures centre on eyes, faces and action – which is why large groups, busy backgrounds, and starring cheques should be avoided. If you are taking group pictures, have them doing something. Individual faces will often merge and be unspotable – or so small as to be meaningless. Similarly, a picture of the fundraising activity will be of more interest than a giant cheque giving free advertising to a bank.

■ THINK BACKGROUND

Editors are as obliged to edit (or crop) pictures as they are unnecessary words. So, unless there is something specifically relevant, important and photogenic in the background – reframe the shot without it. Busy backgrounds distract attention away from the purpose of the shot.

■ REMEMBER CAPTIONS?

Right from our earliest experiences of reading we know that photos and drawings have captions. First reading books are drawings with captions simply underneath. A photo without a caption looks unfinished, and you miss a chance to engage the reader's attention in the article that goes with it. Captions should be short, upbeat, and link the photo with the text. For front pages and major features, the headline will sometimes serve as the caption.

Always *use the best picture on the front page* – even if it doesn't link to the main story. Then you *must* use a caption, explaining the picture's relevance.

It is probably better to send your volunteers and correspondents some rolls of film, and ask to *see the contact sheets* rather than have pictures pre-selected for you.

Ask yourself – *what would I want to know from the picture?* Then find a photograph and provide a caption that gives the answer.

Drawings versus photos

Drawings and illustrations provide an excellent alternative to the dubious photograph. They are particularly useful for buildings, complicated equipment, or showing how things work, when accurate reproduction of detail is less important.

Or when you need to emphasise and break up a vital piece of text. A black and white line drawing will often have a stronger effect on the reader, particularly for dramatic events, than will a picture. It involves the reader, by engaging their imagination as well as their interest.

However both a photo and an illustration only have a role if they:

- Add interest for the reader
- Relate to the objective of the piece
- Emphasise some element of the text

Photographs and illustrations should never be used simply to fill space – like the writing they must have a purpose. Whilst important for grabbing the attention of the reader, they are only one of the building blocks on the page that help to get the message across.

Headlines show the way

The craft of writing good headlines probably causes more angst among newsletter editors than any other part of the job. Subheadings are equally important for breaking up the text into easily selected and digested chunks. In that first brief sweep across your page, it is often the photo and headlines that decide whether the reader will read on.

When writing headlines, the safest guide is to imagine that each of your readers has had an operation. This operation is only available through private medical care, and involves removal, tattooing and replacement of the eyelids. The tattoo, through which everything is read from that day on, is WHAT'S IN IT FOR ME ? If that seems overly cynical, think about it.

Every donor and supporter of yours has their own, usually very personal reason why they want to support or be involved with your cause. It may be as simple as the warm healthy glow of having made a donation to support your good work. It may be much more complicated and individual. Whenever the editor loses sight of the personal interaction that is part of a newsletter, they will find it increasingly difficult to solicit any response. Similarly the shock-horror treatment for stories will pay off only in the short term.

The best responders are those who stay with your charity for a number of years, and they need to hear of the positive impact that their money and efforts have and continue to achieve.

'Label headlines', which occur time and again in many newsletters, simply offer the reader the chance to decide not to read on. 'Fundraising News' or 'Message from our Chairman' or 'Report on the Annual General Meeting' all invite the reader to skip to another part of the newsletter, or put it down in favour of doing something more interesting.

Readers focus best on headlines that directly involve them, or indirectly involve them by tweaking their interest in the story. *'Co-opts for your research'* could herald the story of the Co-operative Society's decision to support your work, or *'Rags to Research'* a collection on your behalf by a student rag group.

Encourage the reader into the rest of the article

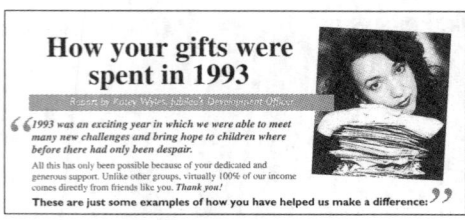

Talk directly to your reader as often as possible

Plays on words are the safest humorous headlines

Headline hints

When working on a headline, ask yourself a few simple questions

■ WHAT IS THE JOB OF THE HEADLINE?

Is it to get attention from thirty feet away or to speed the reader on into the main text? Short sharp headlines work for encouraging the reader on. For most charity newsletters reading on is the key factor. So *'Fighting the floods in Chichester'* would work better than *'Flood alert'*. Better still may be *'How you can help save Chichester'*, which directly involves the reader.

■ WHAT IS THE MESSAGE OF THE ARTICLE?

Do you want to outline a benefit to the reader or to get across some valuable factual information? Key words in these circumstances are quick, solve, help, become or how to. *'How to tell if your child has meningitis'* or *'Solve your benefit problems'* or *'Become a good neighbour to the elderly'*. All have the advantage of sparking the reader's attention when writing of a problem already known to them. Talk to the reader, and build their enthusiasm to read on.

■ CAN YOU USE A QUESTION?

Question headlines, especially using 'you', leap off the page at the reader. For example:

'Could you fly the flag for our awareness week in October?'

Take account of potential answers – if it's not an obvious answer then be prepared to answer the question for the reader or steer them towards the right answer?

'Are you too busy to help on flag day? Ian Botham isn't!'

■ CAN YOU USE A QUOTATION?

Quotation marks around a headline are great attention getters. It is the reading equivalent of eavesdropping. Readers usually want to know who has made the comment and why. A photo, with a caption, can be used to provide that information, or covered in the early paragraphs of the story once you've sparked their interest.

'Soon patients who need a heart transplant will have an alternative' Does this make you want to read on?

■ WHAT ABOUT HUMOUR?

Well, is the story funny? If it is, is it only funny at

somebody's expense? The danger with humour is that it can detract from a serious message, but also appeals in different ways to different people. What will entertain one can insult or embarrass others.

Worse, some readers won't get the joke. The main sources of humour in charity newsletters are unintentional. Usually because the statements made can be taken out of context. Newspapers are no different. Every office has its own favourite list that circulates. Amongst the more famous are:

'PM to act on sex shows!' and *'Pregnant woman told to be more careful.'*

If you were able to write brilliant humour all the time, then a career in copywriting or script writing may be more fulfilling. It would almost certainly be better paid!

Plays on words are less fraught and can work well. The presence of television celebrities can sometimes be parodied with the name of their shows, or catch phrases. A phrase linked to a well known phrase or saying or advertising slogan also works well.

■ IS THERE A HUMAN INTEREST ANGLE?

Good human interest stories tend to be few and far between. Done well, and with the permission of those featured they are excellent pieces that combine a natural interest in people with an underlying message about the work of the charity. They come in many forms. But you know when you read a good one. That's the issue you can't throw into the waste bin, and the story you talk about with friends and family.

Overall it's vital to use simple, key words early in the headline. Remember the aim is to stimulate the interest of the reader. Don't try and tell the whole story in a single line. Otherwise they won't read on. This is a temptation to be resisted for the first few lines of copy as well. The best opening copy is short, sharp, and swings the reader further into the text off the headline. See which style of writing suits the content of the story best – and stick with it.

How to stop writing

Many writers expend huge energy and effort on the first lines of an article, and then run into a creative block trying to finish the piece. Here are some tips to help you out.

■ Finish....ON A CHALLENGE:

Can you do better than this? Tell us if you can.

A Christmas Story

Simon is 7, the youngest of 3 children and severely handicapped. He suffers from an enzyme disorder which progressively leads to brain damage and therefore physical and mental retardation. As a baby he developed normally, but when he was four years old his illness was diagnosed. His body is often stiff and as his illness has progressed he has lost his speech and most of his vision, but if you know him you can tell by the expression on his face if he is happy or not. If anyone from his family – or a voice with which he is familiar – speaks to him he will laugh, or sometimes smile.

Simon recently recovered from a bad cold which nearly took him away. That was the first time I met Simon and his family.

"It is ever so difficult to find a suitable toy for Simon" his Mother says, "And it might be the last Christmas for him, so we want it to be a happy one".

Jill, Simon's Mother, left to go Christmas shopping and I stayed with the three children. His two sisters (aged 8 and 10 years) were eagerly decorating the Christmas tree.

I changed Simon's nappy and tried some of the exercises Jill had shown me to move his body. Very carefully I moved his stiff arms and legs about. Then we had a nice cuddle with Simon sitting on my lap. I put him comfortably down on the sofa and covered him up so he could rest.

I told Simon the Story of Christmas as we watched his sisters decorating the tree. He was very alert and listening – his beautiful dark eyes wide open. Then I had to go upstairs to change Simon's bed sheets and to hang up the washing. The girls called me downstairs to look at the tree. It was indeed beautifully decorated.

Jill came in the door as the girls switched off the main lights and the sparkling Christmas tree lights filled the room. Sharon, the eldest, put on a tape of carols with Simon's favourite Christmas song. We all joined in 'Away in a manger, no crib for a bed...' Jill went to hold Simon in her arms.

"Look" she whispered "he's got tears in his eyes – I haven't seen this for so long..."

Happy Christmas
Elisabeth Braun

A good human interest story will stay with the reader for many months

■ **Finish**....ON A HOOK:

More of Peter's story in a future issue....

■ **Finish**....ON A STARTLING FACT:

Which explains how the decision not to fund the project was overturned!

■ **Finish**....ON A QUOTE:

My wife and I responded 'Your children are our children'

■ **Finish**....BY REPEATING THE LEAD.

Using the headline 'Has your child got a cold or a killer disease?' – the article would finish with 'so now you know what to look for and can decide if its a cold or a killer disease'.

Better sub-headings

Sub-headings are equally vital. Their two jobs are to break up the text on the page, and act as guides or sign posts for the developing story. They can usually be shorter than headlines, but quotations and tweaking of the readers interest are still important.

An article on what happens when you offer to donate bone marrow could be sub headed: the medical; the harvest; the recovery. This splits neatly into three logical sections for the writer. For the reader it is perhaps stronger as:

'What will have to be checked?'

'What will happen in hospital?'

'Will it hurt?'

'How quickly will I recover?'

Editors' Tales

"I suppose dozens of newsletters pass my desk every month. When I was given this job, the first thing I did was call charities and add my name to their subscription lists to see what their newsletters were like. As they started to arrive I read them avidly, made notes on size, shape and colour, article ideas, graphic approaches, and so on.

Most now sit in my post tray unread – or go straight in the bin. When I clear out that tray, I look at each one for a moment and ask myself why I didn't read it. Every answer helps me with my newsletter. Some are just plain boring, no life or bounce to the page. Others are depressingly positive, all life and bounce and no substance. A few I don't recognise because they keep changing the layout.

It makes me wonder what the readers think of my efforts, and look with a fresh eye at each and every page. None of us can afford to be just one more piece of junk mail. Good layout, clear design, and sensible use of graphics will all help sell the story to the reader. They're there to help the writing shine through and get the message across.

Before I add a graphic trick to the page I always ask: will it help or will it look nice? No amount of graphic trickery will disguise empty writing."

When the reader looks at a page of print, the headlines and sub-headings provide the first clues for interest and reading order. Long paragraphs of print, with little white space and few sub-headings are much less attractive to the eye. It is seen as harder reading and needs a greater commitment of time and effort to finish the article.

It is likely that such newsletters are placed on one side to be read when one has more time. Then rediscovered and used to light the fire when out of date! Good headlines and sub-headings grab the readers' interest before that sinking feeling takes over.

Breaking up the text

You can break up the text just by using short paragraphs, white space, and sub-headings. But you will help the reader even more by using bullet points, asterisks, lists, and colour to highlight various points in the text. Much of this is covered later in the chapter on grids, graphics and type, but for brightening up your pages they are vital.

- Bullet points mean less writing

- Asterisks don't need full sentences

- Bullet points highlight part of the text....

- ...but musn't be overused!

A common problem is how and where to use the logo of the charity. One way can be to use it as an end piece for each article. The reader sees it more often, and the newsletter design image is not dominated by having to conform with the logo. Not all logos lend themselves to this use, but some are ideal.

Similarly cartoon line drawings can be used to illustrate articles where photos and artist impressions are not available. Stationers or art suppliers sell reusable copy packs of such items. You can reproduce a cheese shape for an article on foods, or a generic cyclist alongside the calendar for your sponsored cycle ride. Do remember, however, it is very easy to fall into the stereotype trap and fill your page with male police officers and female office cleaners.

Numbers and lists

Rarely used in newsletters these days is the old fashioned, but powerful, list. Used properly the list is an effective tool for getting people to read on. Once a reader knows there are a number of sections to the article, when they begin to read they expect to read all sections. For example:

Five steps to using lists

Step 1: Tell the readers in the subheadings that a list is coming

Step 2: Clearly label, and limit each individual section

Step 3: Readers know when they start they are getting five separate chunks of information

Step 4: Gives brief, clear, recommendations for action

Step 5: Sends them to the response vehicle, or the next section – all about colour!

All about colour

For most newsletters some colour is now almost a necessity. So much other material your readers see is now printed in colour. It is also a help to the reader in both attracting their attention and remembering the information. Tests show that moving from black and white to two-colour presentation enhances retention; from two-colour to four-colour again improves retention.

For most small groups moving up to two-colour print is the step where costs can rise sharply. One way is to simply pre-print the newsletter name plate in colour – rather like a letter head – or a pre placed block or strip of colour on the same pages each time.

Be wary of using coloured paper. Studies show the more you move away from black type on white paper, the harder it is to read the text. After all the other efforts you've made to perk up your pages, don't loose your reader by making it *all* difficult to read by printing on coloured paper.

Glossy presentation?

Smaller charities look jealously up at the budgets of the larger ones, and their glossy magazines of many pages. The short, sharp, punchy newsletter, with few pages, a touch of colour, good headlines, and effective graphic presentation will always get the message across. Many larger charities deliberately choose to under play the glossy approach, and produce simple printed sheets for some of their audiences.

Throughout this chapter, you have seen many examples of newsletter presentation, from which three lessons can be drawn.

- Most of the mistakes you can make have already been made by others

---

Now Decide...

- Is your most important story on the front page?
- Do you use the best photograph on the front page?
- Got a tips sheet and film for your photographers?
- Are your headlines lively and interesting?
- Use a lot of sub-headings on the page?
- Do you vary how the articles finish?
- How expensive does the news-letter look?

■ There are very many successful newsletters, warmly welccmed by their readers – and many that could do a lot better!

■ There are no rules – guidelines yes, but rules no.

Sometimes editors do it all wrong and still get an enormous response from their readers!

CHAPTER SIX

STARTING OR RE-LAUNCHING YOUR NEWSLETTER

One of the key factors in a successful newsletter is building a real identity or persona for the publication. Newspapers work hard at creating an identity, making special efforts to produce features and sectional coverage that matches the profile of their average reader. Look through a range of newspapers the morning after the budget and study the 'average' family impact tables they all use. It will tell you much about who the editor considers the average reader.

> - Is your style and image easily recognised by the reader?
> - Have you spent time and effort developing a name and identity?
> - Do you put the Publisher's Box in the same place each issue?
> - Does each page use the same underlying grid?
> - Will your front page lure the reader from twenty feet?

The nameplate

Of all the building blocks used for identity, the nameplate of the publication is probably most important. Recognising the nameplate and front page of the publication will trigger a recall of past interest and enthusiasm. When you first meet someone, you make instant judgements on appearance, hairstyle, facial expression, enthusiasm, handshake, and name. How often has a limp or clammy handshake made you wary of someone – or massaging your fingers after a vicelike grip a little frightened? So in the newsletter, the first impression is the nameplate. Overlooking this means a lost opportunity to strike a chord in the reader as soon as they pick up the piece.

Thinking about your nameplate

Overwhelmingly, editors decide to place the nameplate at the top of the front page; a minority have the nameplate running down the left hand side; a few elsewhere. The advantage of the left hand side is mainly for publications that are racked in newsagents, libraries or resource centres, when the whole nameplate may then be visible.

It is also tempting to make the nameplate as large as possible, particularly if it is the only spark of colour on the page. But remember, a nameplate is scrutinised carefully perhaps only once or twice.

Think about the example of a first meeting – slowly one starts to recognise the person and where they may differ from or confirm the original contact signals. As those signals are confirmed, or changed, they matter less in how you judge the person after many meetings.

A nameplate can reflect the target audience

A nameplate could strike a positive, lively image

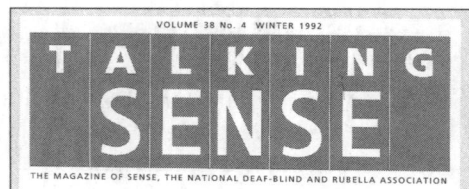

A nameplate can highlight the purpose of the newsletter for the reader

For a newsletter, a striking recognition factor in a nameplate will be important if the memory triggered is that reading it last time was worthwhile!

Three important tests must be applied to the nameplate.

- Does it accurately reflect *content* and *target audience?*
- Does it have a title that fits the group and objective?
- Does it strike a lively, active image with readers?

There are thousands of examples of newsletter nameplates all around you – collect a few and see how they cope with these simple tests. Some words in nameplates show a lack of imagination. So many rely on the word 'newsletter' as part of the main title on the nameplate – whereas 'news', 'focus', 'bulletin', 'spotlight', 'update', 'briefing', 'issues', or 'campaign' strike a much more exciting and positive image.

What makes a good nameplate?

A good nameplate is built around three basic pieces of information:

■ THE NAME OF THE NEWSLETTER

Not the organisation. The newsletter should have an identity in its own right giving readers a feeling of part ownership of this welcome 'letter'. This is the most prominent, visible and memorable section of the nameplate.

■ A SUB-TITLE

Usually with the charity's name and explaining the main purpose of the newsletter. This will be in much smaller type, hopefully not more than 20 words. An amplification of name really, explaining the publisher and aim of the publication.

■ THE DATE

The date, issue number, and any other relevant issue information. You also need to consider whether to use the charity logo or a piece of graphic design that matches and enhances the image of the name. There are many options to consider:

- Colour or black and white for the nameplate?
- All type or using graphic art?
- Does it look too expensive?

It is worth spending time, energy and effort on the nameplate, but do not make it trendy, fashionable, and modern. Fashions change! In two years you'll have to start all over again!

Editors' Tales

"When the committee agreed to a newsletter it seemed a good idea. With five sites, staff scattered over a wide geographical area and working shifts, passing information had always been a nightmare. But the enthusiasm for the idea waned when faced with the practical decisions of writing and production.

The problems started with the name. Whatever seemed bouncy and lively to the office was instantly rejected by the boss. What little life was left on the page was destroyed by our black and white letter logo, and an insistence that the Committee Chairman's message had to go on the front page.

After three issues the print run was 1,000 – remarkable considering it had been intended for our 200 employees! Yet a nagging doubt remained. No-one had ever responded to articles or requests for information in the newsletter. So I went to see what was happening at our largest site.

There were the newsletters in the staff canteen, by the cutlery tray. And sure enough, almost everyone picked one up with their knife and fork. And used it as a table mat that slid into the waste bin at the end of each meal. Any reading was incidental, like the wrappings in an old fashioned fish and chip shop.

The trouble is, someone's got to tell the Committee – because it won't be their fault will it!"

There is a modern trend, beloved of graphic artists, for playing games with type-distorted, extended, even garish lettering, widely spaced and of varied size letters. Forget it unless you are writing for an exclusively teenage audience.

Spend some money now on a classic and simple design. Expect to have to live with the design for at least five years. See it as an investment for the life of the newsletter.

Overall, the nameplate really should not absorb more than 20% of the front page. It's a *newsletter* – the rest of the front page is for your news. Leave space below

Once the nameplate is established, leave it alone

the nameplate, separating writing from the name. Fusing nameplate with the first articles is misleading and reduces the recognition factor. Once the nameplate is done and positioned – LEAVE IT ALONE!

Publisher's Box

The second key factor in building the persona for your newsletter is the publisher's box. This is a simple box of information that gives the reader further details about the publication. People will look for this when they want to contact the editor or know a little more about the source and background of the newsletter. But they will *look* for it. So this is the only box in the newsletter that can be smaller than the basic text type.

If bodycopy type is in 10 point, then the publisher's box can be in 8 point. It should be placed in a regular, unchanging static position, like columns and the nameplate. Readers will probably then see it and scan it on several occasions before they go looking to contact you. It is not news, and should not be placed in prime space, such as on the front or back pages. If you have an inside contacts page or column, that's an excellent place for this information.

Chartown BULLETIN

Volume 1, Number 2 April 1994   4

PO Box 362,
Chartown,
Kent CT12 1BC
01909-110101

The Chartown Bulletin is the bi-monthly newsletter of the Chartown and Volsey Neighbourhood Council, distributed free to the residents of Chartown and Volsey.

Publisher:	Chartown & Volsey Neighbourhood Council
Editor:	Liz Kendrick
Contributors:	Trevor Sharp, Pete Baron, Jane Burt
Editorial Board Members:	Chartown Borough Council; Volsey Residents Association; Chartown Social Services; Volsey Community Health Council

June issue copy deadline: 12th May 1994

Best for urgent, regular information using mainly text

The placement and content of the publisher's box in charity newsletters appears as diverse and varied as the voluntary sector itself. Some are a simple logo and charity address; others an editor's note soliciting contributions; others a list of regional addresses; and a few have no contact spot at all! Putting yourself in the readers' shoes, they may ask a few simple questions:

Question 1: Who is sending this to me?

It is inevitable with the current problems of direct mail, some receivers will instantly try and trace the source of their name and address. All who write to the public face this problem, and with the growth in list swapping and profile selection techniques, it is inevitable that any mailing will generate some queries and complaints.

Question 2 : Why are they sending it to me?

Good question. How well are you targeting your readers?

Question 3: Who is responsible for this?

Who is responsible for the (excellent or dreadful) content? Welcome to the firing line. The beauty of an editor's job is that everyone *knows* with absolute certainty that they could do better – and like to tell you so. However, you will also get calls praising the moving and effective case histories and testimonies that you publish.

Management psychologists preach a motivation technique called the Praise Ratio. They reckon that to balance each criticism you make, you should give eight praise-worthy congratulations. As an editor, it is entirely possible that this principle will be reversed. You will learn to live with this or no doubt change your job!

Question 4: How often can I look forward to re-doing it?

How often will I receive and enjoy or do I have to put up with, this newsletter? The frequency of publication, plus closing dates for contributions is very important information for your reader.

Question 5: Do they really think that?

If this is what they think, they aren't getting any of my money! Contributors will sometimes express views that are different from the charity's stated policy. In fact, good newsletters frequently provoke lively debate about policy changes.

So, now it's clear what basic information must be included:

Answer 1: Name and full address

Details of the publishing organisation, including your charity number.

Please remember the requirements of the 1993 Charities Acts if your newsletter contains any appeals for support. You will usually begin with the name of the newsletter, and the phrase 'is published by'.

Answer 2: A mission statement

The mission statement for the newsletter, which may include a basic description of the target audience.

Answer 3: The Editor's name

The name of the editor and a contact telephone and/or fax number and address, if different from that of publishing organisation.

Answer 4: How often you publish

The frequency of publication, when contributions are required, any brief hints on photographic policy and policy on unsolicited contributions.

Answer 5: Disclaimer

All the views expressed in the publication are individual and not necessarily the view or policy of the charity and its supporters.

In addition, good manners and motivation may lead you to include names of contributors and reporters, certainly any associate editors. Together this information gives the reader a structure and source to the operation of the newsletter, and a feel for the type of publication and organisation that it is, which helps them decide how and where they may wish to get involved. If all that appears in the box is the name of the agency that produced it for you, or the charity's PR or Marketing Unit, ponder what message that may give to the reader.

Size isn't everything...

The size and shape of the newsletter is important for the reader. Newsletters come in all shapes and sizes – multi page A5; 4 page up to 32 page A4, A3, and up to tabloid newspaper. Obviously, the larger the format, the fewer the number of pages you will need for the same information. Remember that pages come in multiples of 4, and there may be a most economic format depending on the size of the printing machine being used. The decision on size and shape is a complex matrix that includes budget, your time, the equipment you use, the skill, source and number of contributors, availability of photographs, printing method and the overall image required.

In addition, think about how and where your newsletter may be read. Does it need to be easily carried, stored or filed? Does it need to stand out amongst other racked items? Bigger or more pages does not always mean better, sometimes simply longer and larger. As a rule of thumb, once you get over 12 or 16 pages, you will probably have to consider advertising to help cover costs, and this changes the whole nature of the newsletter.

It's how you use it!

For subscription newsletters the choice is relatively simple. People pay their subscriptions either because they want to be a member of the organisation and join the cause. The newsletter is of secondary importance. A challenge to the editor to make it interesting! Or they are paying for the relevant information they get from reading the publication. Renewal rates and comments tell you if the information you are providing is full and relevant-readers identify padding items very swiftly.

If you are distributing a free newsletter, effectively paid for from donor funds that could be used directly for the charity's work, then be brief, informative and not too glossy.

The size and shape decision also ties into the underlying grid you use for the design of the publication. A grid is the design shape imposed by vertical columns, margins and horizontal divisions which structures the page layout.

Single-column grid

Here each page is a single column, nearly the full page width. It is perhaps best suited to A5 size newsletters, as it is economical with space. In A4 size, or larger, the mass of text becomes much less inviting, and very long lines of text become difficult to read. Single column format is not very flexible for subheadings and illustrations, so the overall appearance of the newsletter may be unexciting. Use particularly for typewritten newsletters, and to convey a sense of urgency to the information. This information is so important that layout has been deferred for speed.

Single-column, asymmetric margins

The simplest way to sharpen a single-column newsletter, is to use one wide margin, usually but not always on the left hand side of the page. This reduces the length of the lines of text, making it easier to read. It also provides a useful area of white space usable for headings, subheadings and illustrations. If there is a single change small newsletters should consider presentation, this is probably the best one.

Two-column grid

Equal columns running down the page, with the option of spreading headlines or pictures across both. This is easy to manage, and gives a better column length for reading. It is also one of the most frequently used layouts for newsletters. And it can risk looking boring unless handled carefully.

If single-column grids are for newsletters that are mainly text, two-column grids are best for those that have some photos and illustrations available and whose editor has a feel for graphic design. The 'what if' factor on a desk top publishing system allows you to play with layout – but it all takes time and energy.

Single-column grid: best for urgent, regular information using mainly text

Single-column, asymmetric margins: best presentation change for a simple newsletter

Two-column grid: a good simple layout for a mixture of text, graphics and illustrations

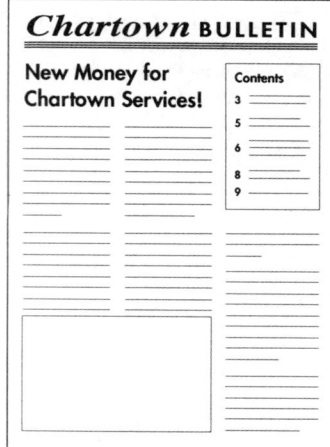

Three-column grid: requires good design skills and some real professional input

Three-column grid

A crisp, active grid for newsletters with several photographs, tables and illustrations to be included on a busy page. Needs generous gaps and spaces between columns and horizontal guides, and a good eye for graphic design and layout. You will probably need some real professional input to create the best design and layout. For more columns, serious professional help is required.

Guidelines for deciding the design

The extra space needed for the best in layout can limit the amount of text you are able to include. The page design will also depend on the size and shape decision. The guidelines could be summarised as:

■ COST

In both time and resources. This is not a drain on resources for each issue. The basic layout decisions are important – but will change very little from issue to issue. The basic grid structure, once selected, remains the underlying design base. This saves considerable time and effort for each individual issue. This helps build the character of the newsletter and improves reader recognition of the publication.

■ IMAGE

You want a clear layout, but not extravagant cost.

■ INFORMATION

The format must enhance the message of the newsletter, not distract with editorial and graphic trickery.

■ EXPERIENCE AND SKILL

Experience and skill in graphic design, and layout that you have at your disposal. The more columns you use, the quicker you will meet complex layout decisions. To produce readable text suitable for a multi-column format requires much greater editorial skill.

■ FUNCTION OF MESSAGE

The function of the message is to educate, inform or draw response from the reader. In general terms, fussy multi-column formats find it harder to create impact.

■ FREQUENCY OF PUBLICATION

The more frequent the publication, the less time you have to edit. It's also harder to limit numbers of pages for infrequent publication. By the time the next issue is ready, some information may already be out of date.

■ PHOTOS AND ILLUSTRATIONS

The more good ones you have available, the more columns you can cope with.

■ USE DUMMIES AND THUMBNAILS

Use dummies and thumbnails as pre-publication layout examples for comment. Before deciding on final format, compare with other publications you like to read and get comments from your colleagues.

■ READING TIME

As the newsletter is read in brief moments of time, think smaller paragraphs and slices of text.

You can also subject your layout to the 'twenty-foot test.' Pin it up on the wall, next to several other publications of the same size, and see which one attracts the eye best. Good grid layout and use of white space will tell the reader early about the time and effort needed to read the piece.

When they start out, many charities simply type under a letterhead on a single sheet of A4. Excellent personal and immediate impact. Larger charities have highly professional multi-column tabloid presentations The skill is in judging when your audience is ready to tolerate the various stages in between.

In general, start simple. Not more than three or four times a year, with just a few pages. An A4 format is the most used, as it can be easily read and stored anywhere. You can always get longer, slicker and more frequent when your newsletter has proved successful and you have gained valuable experience. It's much harder to start big and scale down.

Now Decide...

- Is your style and image easily recognised by the reader?

- Have you spent time and effort developing a name and identity?

- Do you put the Publisher's Box in the same place each issue?

- Does each page use the same underlying grid?

- Will your front page lure the reader from twenty feet?

TYPOGRAPHY, GRAPHICS AND UNITY

The type face and size you use is probably the most important design decision you have to make.

The selection of an appropriate type for your newsletter makes it inviting to read and easy to understand. The reader can scan the text quickly, and absorb the message without having to read through the article several times. Poor type simply stops people reading

To the uninitiated, the detail of typography is mind boggling and boring. Type is easy to change, and subject to selection by whim and current fashion trends. The advent of desk top publishing systems has given many people instant access to a wide range of type faces – and a temptation to mix and vary them which is regrettably frequent.

- Does the reader get a feeling of unity from issue to issue?
- Have you a written specification for type guidelines?
- Are you using pull quotes for reader interest?
- Got enough white space on the page?
- Is clip art used to reinforce a point in the text?

Start with the concept of unity. Each copy of the newsletter should be recognisable by its layout, its typography, and its use of graphics. There should be a clear standard used throughout each issue. Same typefaces, similar headline sizes, same bodycopy size, common caption lines, similar graphics, and so on. The reader feels much more comfortable when in the familiar territory of a unified style.

When to make changes

It is important that you remember this concept of comfortable, unified style for the reader as you read books like this. Part of the reason for writing this book is to supply useful tips, often from bitter experience. The temptation for you is to make swift radical changes to your newsletter. DON'T.

Your readership has got used to things as they are. Make only one major change per issue. If you have been publishing for some time, perhaps every two issues. Some may consider re-launching the newsletter altogether. Be careful. Re-launches with a brand new image rarely please your established readership. All of which simply underscores the importance of unity and familiarity to the reader – and why you should work hard to achieve it.

This, of course, dictates that you should use a limited number of typefaces for your newsletter. There are literally thousands of choices but quality of

Readers' Tales

"I always know when they've bought new software or the editors have been on a course. Something changes. But not just anything – always the bit I enjoyed most. I don't know this editor, but when Bill was in charge I could follow his thinking.

This month we had an artist's impression of 3/4 of a building! Now with Bill it used to be the fundraising thermometer – I could see how far we had to go. Then there was the regional round-up – how the different groups were raising money. I'd know if our group was raising similar amounts from similar events. A sort of profit quality control – and a source of new ideas. We'd try events that worked for others. Now all we get is a league table. And with a country area we're always near the bottom.

The information that I want has moved or has gone. Then there was the colour. I'm not as young as I used to be. I can't read print on fancy coloured boxes – it takes too long. And the print is smaller. The old typesetting had straightforward shapes and sizes. Now it changes on every page and my eyes get tired.

My grandson got a computer for Christmas last year and he sent me a birthday card he made himself. He was trying to show me just how adaptable and useful his new toy was. Inside the card looked like a ransom note from an old detective film; fun – but you're not meant to read it for information. Information should be organised and easy to read.

I'll give the newsletter another six months. I can get the information I want from the regional office. They tell me they're getting a few phone calls like mine each month, asking for information. Next month they're typing a list of fundraising events to photocopy if required. Perhaps I could send them a copy of Bill's old newsletter to show then what else I need..."

appearance and readability depend on consistency of presentation. You have spent much time and effort collecting features, news stories and the content for your newsletter, so the two vital things to get right are readable body copy and headlines that grab attention. However, the type family you put on the page, whilst it must be readable, says something about your image to the reader as well.

Looking at type

Type initially divides into two basic sorts, called serif and sans-serif. Serifs are the tiny lines, or little hands and feet, that are found at the top and bottom of each letter – typefaces that do not have these lines are called sans-serif. The classic serif typeface is *Times Roman*, sans-serif *Helvetica*.

Serif typefaces (with the hands and feet) are usually recommended as best for body copy and blocks of text. They give the best readability in most cases. For the reader they also give an established almost traditional feel to the newsletter as well.

Sans-serif typefaces are more often recommended for headlines, captions, lists, tables – scannable material. If used in body copy they give a more youthful, lively and active feel to the reader. For most newsletters, a sans-

Serif typeface samples:

Times Roman

Century Old Style

Garamond Light

Palatino

Sans-serif typeface samples:

Helvetica

Franklin Gothic

Univers

serif typeface for headlines and subheadings, plus a serif typeface for body copy is probably best. Do consider what else your readers may see – this is a common classical pattern for much printed material, and is thus familiar for the reader.

Guidelines for choosing type

The next decision is which family of type you will select. Sticking to one family of type for all body copy elements will give cohesion to your newsletter. It is important to build interest and variety on the page by using different sizes and weights of the same family, not by switching typefaces. Photo captions, for example, will often be a slightly larger and bold version of bodycopy type. Make sure that the typeface you choose has all the symbols you may require – accents, punctuation marks, mathematical signs etc. There are whole books to assist you with such decisions.

The general advice here is to :

■ Choose established and classical type families rather than young and trendy ones

■ Once chosen, leave it alone for at least five years

■ Specify, and stick to, the same type sizes for similar items in each issue.

Type size is measured in points, 1 point being 1/72 of an inch. Even the sizes of type you select feed into the other decisions such as grids and layout. If you have a one-column grid A4 format, body copy type should be at least 12 pt in size. Otherwise you will end up with too many characters per line for reading comfort. More than 65 characters per line, including spaces, makes reading more difficult.

For two or three columns, bodycopy should be 10pt or 11pt – 12 pt if you know your readership is older and may contain people with sight difficulties. Or if you haven't got much to say! Increasingly, newsletters are using an average bodycopy size of 11pt, rather than 10pt. Whatever, do not be tempted to drop below 10pt if you want people to read it.

Size and space matter

Similarly decide in advance the sizes for major headlines, secondary headlines, fillers, sub-heads etc. And stick to this plan it from issue to issue. It all helps with unity, cohesion and image. Everyone has seen the 'look what I got for Xmas' style of presentation. A new DTP system that can print 37 different typefaces – and most of them feature on every page! 't looks, and is, both amateur and a thorough hindrance to easy reading.

The space between the lines is called leading (pronounced 'ledding') and is also measured in points. In general terms, the longer the lines of type the more leading you will require to space out the line for easy reading.

Leading

The problem with poor leading is that it makes life much harder for the reader.

Smaller gaps between lines can often end in fusion, where the ascenders and descenders of the lines of type meet. The result is confused letter shapes and harder reading. And remember, this is optional reading – if you make it harder to read, the reader will simply move on.

See what we mean?

Single-column grids will need up to 3pts of leading per line – two and three column grids 2pts. Standard defaults on DTP systems tend to be 10/12 (10pt type with 2pts of leading).

Experiment and compare a few pages to see what looks right for your design and layout. In the English language, the most comfortable line length is about 10 words per line – aim for it whenever you can. You should never be tempted to reduce type size or leading to fit more copy on the page – edit it more savagely or leave something out for the next issue.

Leading contributes to the white space on each page. Good, clear designs will try and achieve about 50% of the page as white space. Remember, white space isn't just between lines. It's there between paragraphs, between columns, and all margins. It's above and below headlines, sub-heads, tables and illustrations.

Helping reading

Reading is a muscular and rhythmic activity. To feel comfortable with a page of text white space is important to the eye. It is similar to the difference between driving on a motorway as it should be, and driving as you so often have to, hemmed by too much traffic, too little space and feeling tense and uncomfortable. You keep driving because you have to reach your destination, but newsletter reading is optional!

Be quite clear about this. No-one will ring up and congratulate you on putting more leading and white space in to your design. But you may just detect a few signs of extra readers and increased comment for the newsletter – proving that you're keeping more readers longer.

The advent of word processing and DTP systems has given editors the freedom over a whole range of decisions – often thought to be down to personal choice and preference.

One of the most common and easily changed is the justification of the text. Your text can begin from a straight (or flush) left margin, and either finish with a straight line right margin (justified text) or a ragged line right margin. Each possible design combination has its supporters and detractors.

To justify or not to justify

To have good readability and encourage the reader to stick with the article, it is a mistake to set the body copy in a unusual way. So ragged left is a thoroughly bad idea. Almost everything that is printed in English starts from a straight left hand margin.

It is also increasingly common to see paragraphs that start from that left hand margin, and are not indented. If you are doing this, leave extra white space between paragraphs. This can be a full line, or much less. Indented paragraphs do seem to be slightly better for readability than spacing the paragraphs. Right margin justification may possibly cause two problems.

- Justification can alter the image of your publication. It produces a more formal look, and fits well with a serious, important document, that requires large and difficult decisions.

- By altering the spaces between the words, there is a less rhythmic pattern for the reader, and one can get rivers and lakes of white space which can make reading more difficult. This will be particularly the case for short column widths.

As a newsletter should be lively, interesting and easy to read, justification for right margin seems unnecessary, indeed positively damaging. But this is really a matter for the editor.

Justification decisions affect the whole page, not just the body copy. Headlines, for example, can be ranged left, justified or centred. As can 'call outs' – quotes or key information extracted from an article

Symmetry (centre everything) reeks of boring, unimaginative editing and image; justified established, comfortable, and secure (slightly less boring!); ragged right, friendly and personal. It is possible for you, as editor, to choose any of these options. Given the nature of a newsletter, and its personal, punchy informal style, the correct choice is obvious.

> **Right Margin Justification:**
>
> Almost everything that is printed in English starts from a straight left hand margin. Justification decisions affect the whole page, not just the body copy.
>
> **Ragged Right Margin:**
>
> Almost everything that is printed in English starts from a straight left hand margin. Justification decisions affect the whole page, not just the body copy.

Compare and contrast!

Typographic tips

There are some basic rules to help you decide your newsletter's typography and design:

- Make all basic decisions for typography at the start and stick with them.

- Use two typefaces, one for body copy (serif)

- Use one typeface for headings (sans serif)

- Print flush left ragged right

- Choose sizes for your body type and a hierarchy for the headlines, and for other components of the printed page, and stick with the guide. For example:

Main headline	36pt (bold)
Secondary headline	24pt (bold)

Sub-headings	18pt (bold)
Fillers	16pt (bold)
Captions	13pt (bold)
Body copy	11pt

- Provide plenty of leading and white space on the page and between columns

- Check line length with column width – best between 45 and 65 characters per line

- Avoid italic, condensed, and expanded type settings – they slow the reader down

- Don't centre headlines, flush left and ragged right as per body copy

- Doing all this in advance lets you truly concentrate on the vital element – the content.

Editors' Tales

"Once in a while, a real challenge to your skill comes along. When an organisation cuts its staff and operations for lack of budget, that's one thing. When it consciously decides to make staff redundant, in order to work in a different way altogether, that's difficult. Add to that a Chief Executive who writes twelve words when two would do – and a justifying insert by the accountant showing how the figures work – and you probably wish you were on the redundancy list!

Think first principles. It's news, so it has to go on the front page. Staff and client comments are important, so a sidebar of quotations must be there. Photographs are useless. Nobody shakes hands over redundancy cheques, and long service awards are suddenly a two-edged sword. The essence of the story is a positive step forward to helping more clients in a different way. Balanced by the sad loss of old friends who have given years of service.

The basic message comes from the speech to the staff meeting – good strong quoted headline combining grateful thanks and a positive look ahead. Then the sub-headings to signpost the stages of the debate. Then the four bullet points that measure the better service to clients now on offer.

The sidebar of comments, mainly in favour, but one or two bitter at the loss of their jobs. Then the list. The Six-Step Programme to maximise redundancy benefit and help look for alternative work. Now it makes sense. The reader can see the good things and the problems. Finish with a link to an inside page spread. A Day in the Life of an established client in a residential home, and a new client being cared for in the community, with appropriate photographs.

I can expect a lively letters page for a few issues, and a series of articles on the history of the excellent things achieved in the homes as they close. And the bosses' words of wisdom? They'll tell you later that you entirely caught the essence of their message.

Keep even dramatic news in your standard formats. Use graphic devices to chart your readers' path through the debate. In a time of change, the unchanging presentation and comment of the newsletter can itself be a form of stability. Don't shock – explain. Don't beautify – identify. Remember, GED stands for Graphic *emphasis* device. A way to improve impact for the reader."

Highlighting with graphics

The graphics you use to illustrate and promote the message in the text is another vital area for early decision. What items your system is able to use, and how each element is used to help the newsletter achieve its goals.

Graphics can:

■ Help reduce text

■ Create a better visual format

■ Separate and highlight parts of the message

■ Direct the reader's attention where you want it to go first

■ Develop an eye path for the reader

■ Convey mood and identity

Good graphics, like classical type standards, can enhance the professional image of the newsletter. Poor graphics look not only amateur, but can convey a confusing message to the reader. The illustrations you select will reinforce the editorial line, and may change the perceptions of the reader.

Lines, borders, dividers and boxes

Known as rules, these are amongst the simplest and most effective graphics. Avoid the home made rules – created by constantly repeating an asterisk or a dash. If using a typewriter, use dry transfer lettering or artists pens to put lines and boxes on the page. The majority of word processing and all DTP systems allow use of rules. You can also select width in point sizes.

As with type, do not try and use many different boxes and lines. Limit yourself but use different thicknesses of line and size of box to change emphasis and build interest. With boxes, the fashionable trend is to create shadow boxes. But far too often the shadow box becomes the only box used. A shadow falls behind every outline and drawing in the publication – and loses all impact. Vary and limit each graphic trick.

Tints

If you are producing a two-colour newsletter, then you can use a tint of your second colour in certain areas. Tinted blocks are useful for areas such as nameplates or contents tables; they can add an extra dimension to drawings; and assist with the presentation of data for diagrams, graphs and calendars.

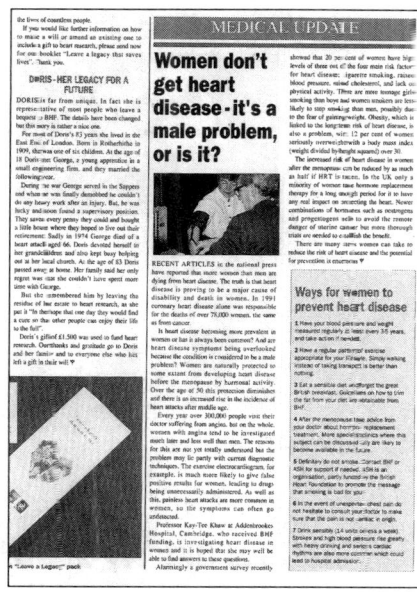

A simple box and numbered list combine to emphasise the main points

A 15% to 20% tint of any colour is usually about right; 10% will often look wishy-washy; over 70% a solid block of patchy colour. Most printers can supply tint charts for you to judge the best percentage for your purpose. You can lay tints for yourself on your DTP system. Single colour publications will often do this with grey to try and add some variety to the graphic presentation. Or you can supply the printer with a disk – you need to check the efficacy and compatibility of your system with the printer's equipment. Or you can ask the printer to lay the tints when making the plate. This is done at the film stage and you need to supply clear instructions for the areas you want the tints to cover and the density of the tint.

Tints are achieved by printing a matrix of small dots in place of a solid block of colour, and measured by the percentage of paper covered by the printed dot. The smoothness of the result is determined by the number of dots per inch a system can achieve. Remember two things:

1. Printers lay tints with excellent equipment and years of experience behind them.

2. When you bought your system, you were probably told it could do tints standing on its head – no problem. Speaking personally, I'm still looking for the machine's head, so I can stand it on it!

Printing on tints

It is very important to think carefully before overprinting body copy text on tinted boxes. It is best to have either a very light tint or emboldened text in such areas. With a heavier or darker tint the temptation is to reverse out the text – i.e. white print on dark background. Reversing out is a very popular trendy trick, much beloved of the current design fraternity. Be very careful. Reversed out type in a large block gives readers a headache and stops them reading. Keep it for sub-headings of only a few words!

Rules, tints and reverses can together create some excellent graphic effects for newsletters. If you are using a second colour, this can be successfully used for rules, borders and boxes, as well as tints. Sub-headings can be printed in the colour, and sometimes, but less often, headlines. Using simple graphs and charts also helps convey statistical information in a more accessible format for the reader.

When to use charts and diagrams

Three dimensional pie charts can show income and expenditure very effectively, and can be shown as divisions of a pound coin, for example. However, do limit the number of divisions – more than eight slices of cake is impossible to digest!

Diagrams should only attempt to show fairly broad movements or changes. For an academic audience, graphs and tables are a way of life.

For the average reader pie charts, bar charts and graphs are the best way to show trends and changes.

Even then, limited colours mean limited numbers of options on bar charts. Avoid confusing charts with a variety of grey hatching to demonstrate different sectors on a bar chart.

'Quoting for emphasis'

One graphic trick still under used for newsletters is the 'pull quote' or 'call out'. Extracting a juicy quotation from the article, and using graphic enhancement through quotation marks provides a hook for the reader. They are very important for copy heavy text where perhaps pictures and other graphic devices are not available.

Use a bold face version of body copy type or preferably subheading size headline type, to print a very small extract from an article. It doesn't always have to be a direct quote from an individual. Part of the editor's job is to spot call out opportunities as they edit the text. In a recent article about a residential care programme, the pull quote in the middle of the article stated:

'Sometimes I think we should close all our centres tomorrow....'

As the article was written by the charity director, one dug deep into the article to see how the sentence finished – 'if we cannot improve on the experience of hospital'. A reasonable point made important and attractive by good editing and graphic emphasis.

Similarly sub-headings are vital in breaking up copy. Each story should have one main headline but several subheadings, a short sharp guide, to what is in the next paragraph. Usually a bold version of the body copy typeface, plus 1 or 2 points, they introduce more white space to the page. And allow the reader to scan the guts of the article very quickly and assess which parts they want to read in full.

Promotions and clip art

Charity newsletters use promotion boxes for information about events, booklets, or T-shirts, pens, raffle tickets offers, usually to good effect. They are a good graphic device for breaking up columns of text and adding variety and interest to the page. Do use them, but limit yourself to one promotion box per four pages of newsletter. Avoid the whole thing taking on the feel of an advertising vehicle.

How your donations are helping to beat heart disease

Dividing up the heart-shaped cake!

Simple clip art hammers home the message

There is a temptation when a chunk of white space surfaces to fill it with a piece of ready drawn or clip art. These are numbers of small drawings or cartoon figures available for re-use sold in copy books or on computer disk. The criteria for use is simple. If you can add impact to an article with a relevant piece of clip art, that makes sense. Even then clip art collections can date very quickly. The number of men seen in clip art collections with kipper ties and flares can be a real source of amusement!

Never, ever, use clip art to fill space. The drawing will lack relevance and may hinder the real objectives of the writing being clear to the reader. Pick up any newsletter just prior to Christmas and count the red suited figures, stars, reindeer and gift boxes lurking in the margins.

When to use a graphic device

The graphic devices you select should pass three tests.

Test 1: Do they enhance understanding?

Test 2: Do they inform more quickly?

Test 3: Do they attract the reader by adding variety to the page?

If they don't qualify under these headings, are they really needed, or are you just showing what your system can do?

Now Decide...

■ Does the reader get a feeling of unity from issue to issue?

■ Have you a written specification for type guidelines?

■ Are you using pull quotes for reader interest?

■ Got enough white space on the page?

■ Is clip art used to reinforce a point in the text?

CHAPTER EIGHT

WHAT DO YOUR READERS THINK ?

In the end, there is no better test of the success and importance of your newsletter than asking your readers what they think. The best design, the straining for readability, the editing, the graphic emphasis, is all aimed to enhance the content. Finding out if the content is what your readers want to read, and if they've read it, is a task that cannot be ducked. It is the real test for creating a successful newsletter.

- When did you last survey your readers?

- Will an Editorial Advisory Board help or hinder feedback?

- Are you regularly seen at conferences and gatherings?

- So, are you achieving those goals?

1. Getting feedback

Surveying all your readership is a time consuming and expensive process, so perhaps first one should look at when it may be necessary.

2. If you already have

- A range of representative focus **groups** from different regions and sectors of the readership, who gives you regular feedback?

- Readers who regularly **comment** and send information?

- Frequent demands and **questions** from readers if you miss a publication date?

- An **Editorial Advisory Board**, with areas of reader interest represented and which is frequently changed to bring in new views?

If you do, you already have a lot of feedback. You may be able to consider fuller readership surveys much less frequently.

A reader survey

But there is no real substitute for a full questionnaire survey sent out to each reader in an issue of the newsletter. There are a number of simple guidelines to take into account.

■ DESIGN OF THE SURVEY

Design the survey with tick boxes, circles and multiple choice questions that allow for computer or scanned marking. This is simply a time and effort saving device that helps you analyse the results.

Chartown BULLETIN

Welcome to October's issue of Chartown Bulletin and once again thanks to those of you who have sent contributions and comments. All are gratefully received and considered carefully for inclusion in the newsletter.

I would appreciate more feedback on the newsletter itself – content, presentation – anything. Just convince me you're out there and reading it!

Trevor's still awaiting your suggestions for the 10th anniversary celebrations. There's a weekend holiday waiting for the successful idea so do get in touch.

The copy date for the Christmas issue is 10th December.

Liz Kendrick – Editor

Give the reader a chance to talk to you

Editors' Tales

"Of all the tasks connected with being an editor, it's talking to readers that most frightens me. They all think they own a bit of your work. And for every one that wants a change there's another who doesn't, and a third who's not sure. When the committee suggested an Editorial Advisory Board, I jumped at the opportunity.

Now I had a smaller group to talk to, who understood some of my problems and were in touch with the readers themselves. They could act as a filter or buffer, quashing readers' wilder ideas and seriously considering the rest. Each department was represented and getting the local newspaper editor to join us was a stroke of genius.

Except he was never there. His own schedule was so tight he was always sending apologies or a deputy. Usually a trainee reporter whose main ambition was to be a crime writer for a national tabloid. Of the others, over several meetings it became clear their main aim was to measure success by column inches of stories about their own departments.

It was the Membership Co-ordinator who said come to the conference. It was a northern group event, and I was surprised to find the newsletter was the only stall in the foyer. More surprised to find so many people wanting to speak to me. Their lists of likes and dislikes about the newsletter were long. But two things were quickly clear. They read it and they wanted it to succeed.

Slowly the Editorial Advisory Board changed. Fewer desk jockeys from head office departments. More local representatives. More stalls at more meetings brought new blood, new ideas, and reporters and writers from all over the country. Formal readership surveys followed and the results sparked further comment and interest.

Be careful. An Editorial Advisory Board can block communication as well as promote it. A newsletter editor stands at one end of a two way street. Anything that acts like a traffic light stopping the flow of traffic towards the editor is dangerous. It gives you a false sense of security as the comment, like the traffic, forms a queue. Much better to allow a free flow and exchange. Even if the readers who comment don't like all you do, it's important enough for them to care to comment. And that's a good base from which to build real success for both the newsletter and its readers."

The first test of the interest your readers have is in the number of responses to your survey request. Magazine surveys will often get a return rate of 2–3%. If you design your survey correctly, and readers think the newsletter is important to them, then 20% plus response rates are not uncommon. With a distribution of 4,000, that is 800 surveys to assess. So think computer marking for your own sanity!

■ FORMAT OF THE SURVEY

Contain the survey on a single sheet of A4 that takes no more than five minutes to complete. Include a brief space at the bottom of the form for general comments. If you box this space, most people will limit their comments to that two or three lines. Some will still attach ten pages telling you exactly what they think!

At the start of the survey tell the reader it takes only a few minutes to complete. And be sure it does. Before you send it out, subject your survey to the ten year old test. If an average ten year old can read and complete the survey in the promised five minutes, send it out. If not, or if any questions cause trouble at this stage, rewrite them.

Chartown Bulletin

Readership Survey

Dear Reader,

We are asking for your opinion about Chartown Bulletin. We would like to take just five minutes of your time to complete this survey. Your comments will help us to improve the Bulletin, and include only the items we know you want to read. This is an anonymous survey, but you can add your name if you wish. But do return the survey to one of our shop collection points by the 20th April. We will publish the results in our June issue. Thank You!

1. What is your opinion of the Chartown Bulletin?

    ☐ very interesting   ☐ quite interesting   ☐ not interesting   ☐ never read it

2. Which features do you read first?

    ☐ news   ☐ features   ☐ advice   ☐ events   ☐ sports   ☐ leisure

3. Which features do you like the most?

    ☐ news   ☐ features   ☐ advice   ☐ events   ☐ sports   ☐ leisure

4. Which features do you like least?

    ☐ news   ☐ features   ☐ advice   ☐ events   ☐ sports   ☐ leisure

5. Who else reads your copy of the publication?

    ☐ family   ☐ friends   ☐ work colleagues   ☐ nobody else

6. Any comments or story ideas you may have?

    _____

    _____

    _____

    _____

Thank you. Look out for the results of the survey on our next issue.

Enjoy reading the rest of the Chartown Bulletin.

■ READER ANONYMITY

Offer readers anonymity. An option to fill in name and contact address if they wish can be included. But point out they don't need to use it. Surveys that offer anonymity will always get higher response rates than those that insist on names. People simply do not like to be linked with criticism, and will be more honest in their comments if they feel there may be no comeback. Similarly postage paid return, or drop off points in offices and shops, giving ease of return are important to the reader.

■ PUBLICISE THE SURVEY

Publicise the survey in advance and set a clear deadline for its return. At least one, and possibly two issues prior to the survey, tell the readers what you're going to do. Simple phrases like 'We want to hear from you, our readers', tagging a brief paragraph may be enough. Certainly the best place to publicise the survey is in the newsletter itself.

Chartown BULLETIN

Have your say!

We are planning a full readership survey for the Chartown Bulletin. Here is your chance to tell us what you think about the newsletter and its contents.

What out for the loose insert in our April issue. Take it out, fill it in _ it will only take a few minutes of your time – and send it back to us by the 20th April. There will be collection points in most of the Chartown shops for the week 13th–20th April.

Don't miss your chance to have your say about the Chartown Bulletin – your local newsletter.

Publicise the survey in advance

Included in the publicity should be a clear promise to publish significant results from the survey. Anyone who has taken part in a poll will know the feeling of looking for the results in the relevant newspaper. Did your opinions agree with others? Are your thoughts and comments in line with the mainstream?

Clearly publishing the results creates a better sense of participation and belonging to the responding group. Even those whose answers are a minority view are reassured by published results – they know that their views have not been ignored, they are merely currently in a minority.

■ USE MULTIPLE CHOICE BOXES

Use multiple choice, yes/no, and numbered ranking questions. Give everybody reading the survey the same range of possible answers. Yes/no, multiple choice and ranking questions get the highest response rates – they require relatively little effort to fill them in.

With multiple choice questions do ensure there is an even number of answer boxes – 4 or 6 is usually best. Survey and examinations tests show that if 3 or 5 boxes are used the middle box tends to attract the constant majority – sitting on the fence! Make the reader choose their answer – don't give them the 'middle of the road' option.

Ranking questions allows people to measure their support for a particular section, article or idea. Scales may be numbered, or from *'usually read'*, through *'sometimes'*, *'occasionally'* or *'never read'*, or the levels of *'agree'* and *'disagree'*. You can judge which parts of the newsletter are best read and loved with careful questions. One newsletter undertook a survey to 'prove' that they should chop the editor's column. From the survey she discovered it was the article readers turned to first in each issue. Remember – readers know best!

■ INSERT THE SURVEY IN THE NEWSLETTER

The best response for surveys come from those inserted as an additional loose sheet in a particular issue. Inserts work better because they do not require the reader to cut up the newsletter, and avoid the editorial decision of whose article is inevitably lost on the reverse side of the page.

Some editors spread the survey over a double side, including folding to prepaid postage return. There is some evidence, however, that trying to fold and return those pages causes your reader more irritation, a search for sellotape (which isn't needed), and worry than they are often worth!

The danger of the insert is the well-established habit of shaking newsletters and magazines over a waste bin after opening and prior to reading. This is only a problem if you regularly carry inserts in the newsletter. The pressure to carry colleague's and advertising inserts for the money this will bring you, is however, undeniably present! Overcome this by referring to the survey within the newsletter itself – preferably as a front page news item-to alert those who don't get it or have already lost it. However, do be prepared with back up copies for phone calls.

> ### *Chartown* BULLETIN
>
> **Tick those boxes – today!**
>
> With this issue of Chartown Bulletin there is a reader survey. Your chance to tell us what you think of the newsletter.
>
> The survey is anonymous – so feel free to say exactly what you think. We'll publish the results in our June issue, so you can see if your opinion agrees with those of other readers.
>
> Don't delay – tick those boxes today!

Use the survey as a news item

■ USE DINGBATS

On the survey sheet itself use 'dingbats' or small images to show ticks or pens. It will help nudge the reader into filling in the appropriate items.

■ OFFER A REWARD

Getting something in return for filling in the survey can enhance responses. It may only be a free draw. One editor recently offered a hundred free subscriptions to the newsletter for the first hundred replies to reach the newsletter offices. A sleepless week followed when he realised that if less than 100 came back, this delivered a resounding judgement on the magazine!

■ USE COLOURED PAPER

If they require nothing else, surveys require confidence in the publication. If using an insert a coloured sheet of paper for the survey will help it to stand out as being different, and needing attention. Some occasionally use day-glo orange or light green. Remember though, such colours can be hard on the reader's eye. A pale colour is much better.

> **Dingbats**
>
> Use dingbats to nudge the reader into action
>
> ✂ scissors   ✄ scissors
>
> ☎ telephone   ✈ airplane
>
> ✍ hand & pen   ☞ hand

If you have got this far, and like the concept of a survey, but would find it hard to cope with an avalanche of returns all at once, try a rolling survey. Survey perhaps 10% of the readership, at random or alphabetically, over four issues. It is more difficult to pre-publicise, but easier to handle in terms of volume. If the publicity is handled by insert as well it is feasible.

If you opt for a rolling approach, do not make changes to your format until three surveys give similar requests for change. It is hard to make a rolling survey work well if you publish quarterly. Monthly or bi-monthly issues will give a sensible result in six months – if readers wait a year to see results, they'll have forgotten what they said!

Talk to your readers

There is another opportunity to sample reader thinking, during annual or regional conferences, meetings and sometimes events. Usually the newsletter will have a correspondent attending or some other method of covering what's happening. But particularly at an AGM or equivalent, put up a newsletter table, go and mix in the foyer wearing a big badge and talk to delegates about the newsletter itself. Take the clipboard and sample the views with a few simple questions.

At events you may also get quotes and a chance to follow up celebrity attendants for interviews or feature stories. Just be there, be obvious (the clipboard helps), and be proud of your publication. You may just be pleasantly surprised at what your readers think of your 'baby'!

Chartown BULLETIN

A real vote of reader confidence

In this issue we report our readership survey results. Hundreds of you ticked the boxes of the survey and put them in our shop boxes. Overall you told us that the news, events and sport coverage of your own local newsletter was important to you.

Thank you! Its great to know so many of you read and support our efforts. Turn to page 4 for the full survey results.

Readers like to see survey results published

Using the results

When the results come in, and you've fed the basic answers through the computer you must set aside time to assess the comments. With a colleague, for speed and support, set aside an afternoon – listing general comment areas, but most important, note interesting or erudite phrases. One of the best parts of writing up a survey is creating the 'commentary' paragraphs that follow the survey statistics.

Make sure you've discussed the survey results fully in the office and with your sponsoring organisation before you publish the results. If you can plan changes or additional items as a result, this may give you an excellent opportunity to write an editor's column telling the readers which items are being changed, and inviting comments on your plans. Surveys can often begin a

---

Chartown BULLETIN

Feedback – feedback – feedback

We were delighted with the response to last month's request for feedback. Your ideas and examples have kept us busy, and many of your comments are summarised below.

Please keep calling and writing. Your views are always welcome, and the articles in this issue need your comments and suggestions as well.

Turn first to page 4, where our first reader article idea is presented – thanks to Fred Partridge's call only 2 days after our publication date.

Surveys are only one step in maintaining good relations with your readers

longer and more involved communication with your readers.

How often do you need to put yourself through this torture? Probably around every three to five years, or at least once for each editor, if they change more frequently than that! It is an important monitoring process for the newsletter, and helps to demonstrate to the readership that they are a vital element in the conduct of the newsletter.

It also helps you, the editor, demonstrate to your organisation that the newsletter is achieving its goals and objectives. Which is, I think, where we started!

Now Decide...

■ When did you last survey your readers?

■ Will an Editorial Advisory Board help or hinder feedback?

■ Are you regularly seen at conferences and gatherings?

■ So, are you achieving those goals?

SELLING ADVERTISING SPACE

Now you are producing your newsletter, you can consider getting advertising for the publication. This can be either to contribute towards the cost of the newsletter, or to raise additional monies for the organisation.

Initially you need to decide if taking advertising will change the tone and image of the newsletter. It may upset your readers. Remember a newsletter is a unique mixture of personal letters and news. Not many newspapers are as welcome and avidly read as a good newsletter.

If you are unsure as to your audience reaction, then goodwill advertising may be a sensible compromise. Much charity advertising gives little or no benefit to the companies who pay for it. The advertising is taken as a form of support for the charity's work. It is, therefore, the value and measured results of your work, the urgency of the problem or need you are tackling, and the sympathy of those you approach that are the vital selling points. Few amongst your readership will be offended by this type of advertising support, which is clearly a form of 'dressed-up' donation.

However there may be a very good commercial reason why a company might want to advertise in your publication. Your newsletter may be one of a very small number of ways your advertiser can reach a selected audience. Sports companies could well be interested in a athletic club newsletter; a home choice carpet service in a newsletter for the elderly or disabled; equipment companies in a newsletter for playgroups and nurseries.

So, before you go any further, you must look and decide what your newsletter and its readership has to offer any potential advertisers.

> - Is there commercial interest in your readers?
> - Have you an agreed number of pages to sell?
> - How do you approach potential advertisers?
> - What evaluation of response can you offer your advertisers?
> - Can you balance advertising income against direct costs?

Who are your readers?

The first thing any potential advertisers will want to know are some details of your readership. These are the people who will see, and hopefully respond to, the ad. There are likely to be three basic types of readers, which will at times overlap. But each has their advantages and problems for the editor's decisions on advertising.

□ □

Checklist of what you have to offer

Try answering these questions about your publication. From this you should be able to create a crisp sentence or two to describe the publication. This can be useful as a statement for the **rate card**, for a covering letter, or when doing interviews with the local media.

Tick all 'yes' answers

Its readers are:

□ Young   □ Old   □ Middle aged

□ Rich   □ Poor   □ A wide cross section

□ Of various nationalities   □ Other_____

It will cost_____per issue (eg £1.00, 50p, 25p, free)

Print run_____

Estimated readership_____ (eg 10x, 5x, 2x number of copies to be distributed)

It will be distributed through the following outlets (estimate the numbers for each outlet in the space provided):

Newsagents (_____)

Launderette (_____)

Local membership (_____)

Community council (_____)

Local clinic/surgery (_____)

Street corner (_____)

Local market (_____)

Festival/special event (_____)

Door-to-door (_____)

Local radio phone-in (_____)

British Legion/WI etc (_____)

Citizens' Advice Bureaux (_____)

College/university/schools (_____)

Other _____ (_____)

_____ (_____)

_____ (_____)

■ A COMMITTED READERSHIP

Perhaps the most difficult group to 'sell' to and the easiest to upset. It is support for the cause, commitment to action, interesting articles and relevant information that keeps this audience reading. They expect the same level of belief and commitment from the organisation and its publications. And may quickly stop reading if too many ads invade this communication that is so important to each and every reader. A limited amount of goodwill advertising to assist with costs may be as far as these readers will tolerate such intrusion.

■ A SPECIALIST READERSHIP

A small group usually, but one that may be difficult to reach, which makes up for its lack of numbers. A newsletter aimed at chess players, for example, will appeal to chess suppliers, but what about suppliers of short break accommodation in tournament towns; cheap travel offers; perhaps even air cushions! The simple question is 'what do our readers need?' For this group, relevant advertising will add to the appeal of the newsletter.

■ A LARGE, MORE GENERAL READERSHIP

Your readers have something in common because they read your newsletter. They may have a geographical connection - they live on a particular housing estate or are members of the same church congregation. Your selling point here is that you cover a local area, and at much lower cost than commercial newspapers and magazines. Plus general readership object less to advertising in the newsletter. Perhaps they don't read it at all, anyway! Your disadvantage is that the group may be so diverse that it will limit potential advertisers' interest.

Whichever group represents your readers, you need information about them – who they are; how many are there; what their interests are: what they want to read or buy. Any newspaper or magazine will want to feature advertisements for the goods and services their readers use. The type of advert you see in *The Daily Sport* would not appeal to readers of *The Daily Telegraph*. Not usually anyway!

Looking at reader habits

The last chapter dealt in some detail with the principles of reader surveys. If you are going to sell advertising as well, then you may have to add some questions about reader habits (reading matter; television and radio habits; hobbies and leisure interests) and personal details (marital status; age; occupation; education; income level).

Remember that this does not always cover all readership. Many small circulation newsletters are read by more than the recipient alone. They are in doctors' waiting rooms, libraries and places where many others may scan the contents. This is difficult to quantify, but is very important information for advertisers.

A reader survey

The more you know about your readers the easier it will be for you to sell your advertising. This can be particularly important where you have a specialist readership or a wide local readership. The survey printed here is adapted from a membership survey undertaken by Friends of the Earth. You could create your own readership survey by adapting the questions to fit your own circumstances.

The questions cover the publication itself, attitudes to it and the readership and its characteristics (which can be deduced from such things as educational background and what publications they read). All questions should be set out with a tick box format for ease of use and analysis. The number of open-ended answers should be kept to a minimum, although you might like to have sections on general attitudes to your publication and suggestions for its improvement.

Please answer the following questions, which will help us produce an even better publication:

About the publication

1. What is your opinion of the publication?
   ☐ very interesting ☐ quite interesting ☐ not very interesting ☐ not at all interesting
   ☐ have never read it

2. Which features do you like most?
   ☐ news ☐ features ☐ advice ☐ events listings ☐ crossword

3. Which features do you like least?
   ☐ news ☐ features ☐ advice ☐ events listings ☐ crossword

4. Do you think the publication is sent too often or not often enough, or are you happy with the frequency of issue?
   ☐ sent too often ☐ not sent often enough ☐ happy with frequency of issue

5. Who, other than yourself, reads the publication?
   ☐ family ☐ friend(s) ☐ member(s) ☐ nobody else

6. What do you feel about the price of the publication?
   ☐ excellent value for money ☐ about right ☐ too high ☐ much too high

About the Association

7. Which issues most concern you? (please indicate order of importance)
   ☐ pollution (___) ☐ recycling (___) ☐ acid rain (___) ☐ North Sea (___)
   ☐ safe energy (___) ☐ Sizewell (___) ☐ countryside (___) ☐ pesticides (___)
   ☐ public transport (___) ☐ cycling (___) ☐ tropical forests (___)

8. Are you a member of, or do you contribute to other campaigning groups or charities? (please specify)_____

9. How effective do you feel the Association is compared with two years ago?
   ☐ more effective ☐ less effective ☐ about the same

About yourself

10. Which of these daily newspapers do you read or look at regularly?
    ☐ Independent ☐ Daily Express ☐ Daily Mail ☐ Daily Mirror ☐ Daily Star
    ☐ Daily Telegraph ☐ Financial Times ☐ Guardian ☐ Sunday Times ☐ none of these

11. Which of these Sunday papers do you read or look at regularly?
☐ Mail on Sunday ☐ News of the World ☐ Observer ☐ Sunday Express
☐ Sunday Mirror ☐ Sunday People ☐ Sunday Telegraph ☐ Sunday Times
☐ none of these

12. Do you read or look at the TV Times or Radio Times magazines regularly?
☐ TV Times ☐ Radio Times

13. Which of these religious publications do you read or look at regularly?
☐ Catholic Herald ☐ Catholic Universe ☐ Church Times ☐ Friend ☐ Methodist
Recorder ☐ Jewish Chronicle ☐ Reform ☐ none of these

14. Which of these magazines do you read or look at regularly?
☐ Resurgence ☐ Cosmopolitan ☐ New Statesman ☐ Spare Rib ☐ Working Woman
☐ Reader's Digest ☐ Which? ☐ Woman and Home ☐ Good Housekeeping
☐ The Ecologist ☐ Sanity ☐ New Scientist ☐ Private Eye ☐ The Spectator
☐ The Economist ☐ New Society ☐ Others (please specify)_____

15. Which are your main leisure interests?
☐ gardening ☐ sports ☐ cycling ☐ keep fit ☐ motoring ☐ cooking ☐ music
☐ cinema ☐ theatre ☐ DIY ☐ knitting ☐ sewing ☐ health food
☐ others (please specify)_____

A few personal details

16. Are you:
☐ male ☐ female ☐ married ☐ single ☐ divorced ☐ widowed ☐ separated

17. Are you aged:
☐ 17–24 ☐ 25–34 ☐ 35–54 ☐ 55–64 ☐ 65–70 ☐ over 70

18. What is your occupation? _____

19. Are you: ☐ working full time ☐ working part time ☐ unwaged ☐ retired ☐ a student

20. When did you finish your education?
primary school (_____) secondary school or 6th form college (_____)
college of higher education (_____) university (_____) postgraduate (_____)

21. What is your total annual household income before tax?
☐ under £5,000 ☐ £5,000–£9,999 ☐ £10,000–£14,999 ☐ £15,000–£19,999
☐ £20,000–£24,999 ☐ £25,000–£29,999 ☐ £30,000 and over

22. How did you vote at the last General Election?
☐ Conservative ☐ Labour ☐ Liberal Democrat ☐ Green Party ☐ other ☐ did not vote

23. How will you vote at the next General Election?
☐ Conservative ☐ Labour ☐ Liberal Democrat ☐ Green Party ☐ other
☐ do not plan to vote

Thank you for your help in completing this questionnaire. Note that the information is confidential and you cannot be identified from the replies you have given.

Please return this questionnaire as soon as possible in the freepost envelope provided.

Production schedule

This is a schedule for a charity event programme required for distribution at the event itself. All schedules should allow the publications to be available when they are required for distribution, with some margin to cater for unforeseen contingencies if possible.

Date of event .... July 30

Picked up by Sales Team .... July 26

Delivery to Central Distribution point .... July 23

Publication printed, bound, packed .... July 20

Editorial conference with Ad Manager and Editor .... July 6

Page proofs to Ad Manager and Editor .... July 4

Deadline for advertisement copy .... June 20

Start selling advertising space .... May 6

Rate card and covering letter mailed out .... April 26

Rate card and covering letter draft agreed .... April 12

Sub Committee formed / Ad Manager appointed .... April 5

Work a production schedule back from the publication date

When talking to advertisers, don't forget that the term newsletter will imply a relatively modest publication. This will limit the possibilities for the type of advertising that will fit with the design and production. Taking a glossy ad and putting it into an otherwise modest publication clearly will do little to help advertisers or the organisation itself. Think how the reader may react – and act accordingly.

How much can you charge for advertising?

For most charities, the answer is 'as much as we can get away with ' But it is quite easy to calculate a break even rate, and then judge how the prices compare with alternative media on offer to advertisers. There are three basic steps to achieving a break-even rate.

Step 1: Calculate the costs of production

At first, an easy task. Printer's quote, plus distribution and basic office costs. But what about the time and effort that's going to be diverted to getting advertising? Telephone calls, artwork, visits, time – all clearly add to costs – or reduce time spent maintaining the quality of content for the newsletter. If all else fails, add at least 25% to your known, existing costs per advertising.

Step 2: Divide this figure by number of advertising pages

This is a real crunch consideration. How much advertising do you need to cover those costs? How much will readers tolerate? Once any newsletter gets above around one third of its pages filled with advertising, readers tend to turn away in droves. Think of the fate of your local free newspaper, usually full of advertising and not well loved or well read.

Step 3: Work out a break-even page rate

This comes from step two, but you must add a margin of 15% to 20% as a contingency. If you don't sell every space, if one advertiser drops out, or you don't get paid!

Only now can you re-visit your original premise to break-even and see if it works. You may settle for fewer pages of advertising, and a contribution to costs otherwise met from your general funds. You must also check your charges are not too far out of line with those charged by similar organisations. It's easy to collect rate cards and other advertising data from local offices.

Dividing the page unevenly

From the page rate, calculate charges for smaller spaces than a page. These should not be pro-rata. To sell one page to four advertisers is at least four times the trouble. A page rate of £200, should break down to two half pages of £125 each (£250 per page), or four quarter pages at £70 each (£280 per page).

You may also have to allow for dealing with a company's advertising agent, who will deduct 15% from your invoice as their commission. Allow for this in your calculations. Unless you are a very local publication, you will meet and have to pay agents. But they will often encourage advertisers

---

Calculating the advertising rate

Here is an example of how to calculate advertising rates on a break-even basis for a 32-page publication in which it is planned to obtain 12 pages of advertising.

Total budgeted production costs (as per printer's estimate plus any overheads incurred in editorial and advertising sales)	£750.00
Divided by 12 (number of pages of advertising)	£62.50
Rounded up to	£75.00 per page
or	£40.00 per 1/2 page
or	£25.00 per 1/4 page

Don't sell yourself short with even division of cost

and handle artwork for you. So accept the possibility and make it work to your advantage.

There are three 'premium' positions for advertisers. The back cover, inside front cover, and inside back cover. If you get you sums right, and sell a four-colour back cover, you may get a four-colour front page for that issue. It all depends on the size and printing format for the newsletter. Parish magazines often only sell these spaces.

Once you get the advertising moving you can mount special features – really just an excuse for approaching companies with a common theme. For advertisers, special features have the advantage of being linked to some editorial copy. It is vital that you do maintain editorial independence and integrity in such circumstances. 'Puffery' discredits publications quicker than anything else. A special feature on transport in a newsletter for the disabled must still be able to criticise companies who get it wrong. Even when they're potentially the biggest advertisers.

For some publications, a page of classified (sold per line) advertisements is seen as a good compromise. It's often an excellent reader service, indeed once established the classified page is sought out quickly by the reader looking for that 'bargain'. But for raising money it's very hard work. Classifieds are viable for a year, or a set number of issues. If each issue has the to be completely re-set, then the time and effort involved will eat away at the money raised.

The rate card

Once you've got a grip on the finances, and the pages available to sell, you'll need to print a rate card. This is the card which sets out all the advertising rates and production information that an advertiser needs to know. Usually sent out to potential clients with a covering letter, after an introductory telephone call, this package must be brief, clear, and concise. The letter with the card should contain a paragraph about the charity and its aims. Be clear about exactly what you want the recipient to do – and by when. And remember, the rate card must include contact name and telephone number. It is inevitable that at some point it will be separated from the letter.

Who will buy?

So, now go sell your space. Personal contacts are almost certainly the best place to start. Gather your committee members together, and give them a deadline to produce twenty names, addresses and telephone numbers each. Plus a line or two on each one about why they might be interested. We all know some people who are in business, especially retail trade, and often the committee members will check first with the named person, thus 'warning' of your approach.

Rate card and covering letter for a periodical publication

Chartown Bulletin PO Box 362, Chartown, Kent CT10 1BC, Tel: 01909 110101

Advertisement Rates 1995

This monthly newsletter is hand-delivered to every household in the borough, keeping 5,000 Chartown residents up-to-date with news, views and events.

Size	A4
Print run	5,000
Readership	estimated 3 per household
Published	last Friday each month
Deadline	for all copy/editorial: 2 weeks before

	1 insertion	6 insertions (per insertion)	12 insertions (per insertion)
Back cover	£180	£160	£140
Inside front	£150	£135	£120
Inside back	£150	£135	£120
Whole page	£100	£90	£80
Half page	£60	£54	£48
Quarter page	£40	£36	£32
Inserts	£50 per thousand		
Classified	£3 per line, 10% reduction for series of 6 unchanged insertions		

Covering letter

Dear_____

On the last Friday of every month, come hail, rain or shine, our team of 150 volunteers push a copies of the Chartown Bulletin into each and every one of the 5,000 letterboxes in Chartown. We know our readers eagerly await its arrival because they write and tell us, telephone us, and stop us in the street to tell us so.

There are many reasons for its continuing popularity – lots of local interest stories, on-the-spot photographs, and our fearless reporting of local issues without political bias of any kind. Our regular features – the crossword, gossip, cookery and gardening columns, the over 60s angle and Young Mums' Forum – have all helped us make Chartown Bulletin Chartown's No.1 Good Read, and we aim to keep it that way.

Advertise your company's products and services with us and get your message into 5,000 letterboxes each month. An advertisement rate card is enclosed with full details. If you have any queries, please don't hesitate to call me.

I look forward to hearing from you, and if I don't – I'll call you!

Yours sincerely,

Alice Jeans
in charge of advertising

> ## Listing contacts
>
> This is an example of a form which might be used to list contacts to approach for advertising:
>
> ---
>
> ### Chartown Resident's Association
> #### Annual Report
>
> Jane Wilshire has agreed to act as Advertisement Manager for the Annual Report, to offset the cost of it being professionally produced. Please write down full details of individuals and companies she can approach for advertising or sponsorship and state if we can use your name as contact.
>
> Your name ————————————————————
>
> | Name/position | Name/position |
> | --- | --- |
> | Company | Company |
> | Address/phone | Address/phone |
> | Comments | Comments |

Get your committee working!

Other sources include files on previous advertisers and companies who have already donated to the charity's work. Trade directories (Thomson's Local or Yellow Pages); Chambers of Commerce lists; Kompass directories; and noting those who advertise in the local press and on local radio. You can end up with a huge list to attack.

But as you attack it, always seek to look at the publication from the advertiser's point of view. Earlier in this book, you were encouraged to think of your readers having had the operation to produce the 'what's in it for me' perspective. This point goes double for advertisers. Could they sell all their goods and services to your readers? Is there a genuine service to both in bringing readers and advertises together? In a newsletter for carers, for example, respite care services, accompanied holidays, doorstep delivery shopping, good neighbour schemes, teleworking from home may all have a place. Look for areas of mutual advantage.

Approaching your prospects

By telephone or in person. Then a letter and rate card either sent on or left with them. Written approaches, particularly sent cold, will end up where most of your office direct mail goes. In the round 'filing cabinet' at the end of the desk. For each and every contact a few simple points are important.

■ DECIDE ON A METHOD OF APPROACH

A link between the newsletter and prospect; a tie in with special features; use of your newsletter by competitors; link to potential buyers in the readership; personal introduction or referral; etc.

■ USE PREVIOUS ISSUES OR A DUMMY

Show the advertisers how the pages may look, where the possible positions in the newsletter may be. Show and tell is always better than just tell.

■ FOLLOW UP AND KEEP RECORDS

Maintain a contact log. Make a certain number of telephone calls each day, check which are sent rate cards, and set deadlines for next contact or visit. Persistence and single mindedness usually pays off. But it's also true that sheer quantity of approaches is at least as important as quality when filling pages issue after issue. You will need a broad contact base. Advertisers tend to be periodic rather than constant supporters.

Can you write advertising copy?

Small companies, particularly retail outlets, will often want to advertise but have no real idea how to put it on the page. Unlike bigger companies, there will rarely be artwork such as other ready made ads to copy. You are much more likely to win their business if you can offer to help write the ad for them.

A few simple tips to help with this process:

■ USE THE COMPANY'S LETTERHEAD

Using this as a starting point will save money for the client, as it requires no new artwork.

■ REMEMBER VISUAL IMPACT

Most advertising relies on few words, impact and image. The majority of your small business clients will want too many words or too much information in their ad. A quarter page ad works best with 30 words or less.

■ EVERY WORD COUNTS

Mostly, full sentences and proper grammar are too wordy. Short, sharp, punchy information works best.

■ PRICES ARE A DETAIL

Unless price is the main theme of the ad, don't include them. Encourage the advertisers to promote on quality, service, tradition, convenience.

■ COUPON ADS MEASURE RESPONSE

The best way to get the advertisers to come back a second and third time is to measure and evaluate the response. Coupons that offer reductions or extras on production of the ad show the retailer quite clearly if the price of advertising was worth it.

Having inserts

An alternative or additional source of advertising income is to use inserts. This is simply a sheet provided by the advertiser inserted loose into each copy of the newsletter (usually by arrangement with the printer). The price you charge must reflect this added cost. But be warned. The commercial rates for inserts vary widely according to what is known about the circulation and the readership. Similarly, more than one insert per issue becomes irritating for the reader, unless you are printing a substantial magazine.

Postage costs can go up with the extra weight of inserts – check with a dummy made of same weight paper if necessary. You must also reserve the right to refuse any insertion that is booked unseen. You should be sure the contents do not give offence, or are inappropriate for your readers. Titles promoted by video shops may not be right for your audience; or loans at high rates of interest for low income groups. Such problems are

---

Editors' Tales

"The first money we raised directly from the newsletter was from a corporate sponsor. A regular company supporter tied part of their annual donation to sponsoring the newsletter. The sum involved didn't begin to cover the cost but it got us all thinking.

During the next year we carried some advertising. Mainly goodwill gestures from businesses that supported the work of the charity. It got tucked into page 3 of the newsletter. When there wasn't enough to fill the space, we either threw in some clip art or gave one of the advertisers a bit more space.

It was in the third year that advertising income appeared in the budget as a target. It was modest, only a little above the previous year's figures - and accepted with little comment in a year when all had to tighten their belts.

But it was also a year when businesses were tightening their belts. It was harder to find easy goodwill gestures. Even then, there weren't the same spin offs from corporate fundraising. In a year when they found it hard to reach their targets, the newsletter was now competition, my responsibility to sell, not something they could throw into their packages anymore.

I sold all the necessary space. But it took time and effort away from other editing tasks, and the adverts were now dotted throughout the newsletter, altering most of the page layouts each issue. And I had acquired a couple of bad debts - one of which was an established corporate donor who'd topped up their donation with an extra piece for the newsletter. I couldn't chase the debt for fear of putting the remaining donation at risk.

Time to do it properly. We took on an agency to find advertisers. Goodwill advertising has gradually faded, and new advertisers have appeared. Twice we've had to turn away adverts in poor taste, once for ethical reasons. The accountant is happy, we're now 50% self - funded by advertising revenue. We're 8 pages instead of 4, with the equivalent of 3 pages of advertising.

But I notice responses are down. Letters and comments are fewer and advertisers sometimes complain about some of the campaigns we run. When I started as an editor I worried about who would write the articles and who would read them. Now I worry about advertising revenue targets and their responders before my own. Somehow that doesn't seem quite right..."

□ □

Invoices

This is a sample invoice which also confirms details of the arrangement:

Invoice

Chartown Bulletin Newsletter

PO Box 362, Chartown, Kent CT10 1BC

June 30th 1995

To: Acme Industrial plc

    42 Wenley Road, Chartown

1 x 1/2 page advertisement in the October newsletter as agreed: £45.00

Please send your copy/camera-ready artwork together with your remittance
to reach us no later than the deadline, 30th August 1995.

The advertisement size and publication details are as specified on the attached rate card.

Reminders

This is a sample statement to send out where payment has not been received:

Statement

Chartown Bulletin Newsletter

PO Box 362, Chartown, Kent CT10 1BC

August 18th 1995

To: Cuddles Babyshop

    15 High Street, Chartown

1 x 1/4 page advertisement in the June issue: £36.00

Please give this invoice your urgent attention
   (one month later)

Please note this account is now overdue
   (two months later)

We shall take steps to recover this amount unless we hear from you within seven days
   (three months later)

Now Decide...

■ Is there commercial interest in your readers?

■ Have you an agreed number of pages to sell?

■ How do you approach potential advertisers?

■ What evaluation of response can you offer your advertisers?

■ Can you balance advertising income against direct costs?

rare – but be prepared. Usually it's a genuine misunderstanding between advertisers' wishes, and your knowledge of the readers.

Getting the money

Confirmation of an advert or insert booked by the advertiser should be by invoice. The arrangement, and its cost, is fresh in the mind of the advertiser, and it helps speed up the payment to you. Most businesses operate on a 30 day credit arrangement, and the earlier you get that income moving the swifter you will get paid.

Smaller charities should insist on payment with submission of artwork and copy. You can then chase for payment at the same time as copy, and this reduces your chances of taking an ad and then not getting paid.

It is not a good idea to send proofs to advertisers for checking unless you really have to. This will create delays, And may also give advertisers the opportunity to change their copy. This is expensive and time consuming. You take responsibility for checking the advertising copy at proof stage. A free ad in another issue is normally a cheaper and more time effective way of covering any errors that creep in.